The World Population Crisis:

POLICY IMPLICATIONS AND THE ROLE OF LAW

PROCEEDINGS OF THE
AMERICAN SOCIETY OF INTERNATIONAL LAW
REGIONAL MEETING

AND

THE JOHN BASSETT MOORE SOCIETY
OF INTERNATIONAL LAW SYMPOSIUM

GREENWOOD PRESS, PUBLISHERS
WESTPORT, CONNECTICUT

Library of Congress Cataloging in Publication Data

Main entry under title:

The World population crisis.

Reprint of the ed. published by John Bassett Moore Society of International Law, Charlottesville, Va.
1. Population--Law and legislation--Congresses.
2. Birth control--Law and legislation--Congresses.
I. American Society of International Law. II. John Bassett Moore Society of International Law.
K2000.A55W67 1980 344'.048 80-19753
ISBN 0-313-22619-9 (lib. bdg.)

Reprinted in 1980 by Greenwood Press
A division of Congressional Information Service, Inc.
88 Post Road West, Westport, Connecticut 06881

Printed in the United States of America

10 9 8 7 6 5 4 3 2 1

Forward

As U Thant has correctly recognized, the most urgent conflict confronting the world today is not one based upon disagreements between nations or ideologies, but rather between the pace of growth of the human race when placed in juxtaposition to the insufficient increase in the resources required to support mankind in peace, prosperity and dignity. Yet, oddly, it has been only within the last decade that the problems associated with population growth have seemed to be a proper subject for human concern.

With this in mind, on March 12 and 13, 1971, the University of Virginia School of Law hosted a Regional Meeting of the American Society of International Law and Symposium of the John Bassett Moore Society of International Law on "The World Population Crisis: Policy Implications and the Role of Law." Geoffrey Keppel and Patricia Otto, prime movers and organizers of the Symposium, succeeded in bringing together scholars, decision-makers, lawyers, and representatives of international institutions to discuss the multifaceted issues relating to the population crisis.

These proceedings are being published, therefore, with the hope that they will provide for the widespread distribution of the innovative interchange of ideas experienced by those who participated in the Symposium. Envisioned also is that this volume will serve to acquaint the reader with the complexity of the economic, political, technical, social, and legal forces which influence the formulation and implementation of population policy.

Charlottesville, Virginia
June, 1971

Editor

John M. Paxman

Editorial Staff

William W. Gearhart, Jr.
Geoffrey H. Keppel
Patricia Otto
James E. Roselle

It is the policy of The John Bassett Moore Society of International Law not to take an official position by resolution or otherwise upon controversial questions. The views expressed in the addresses and remarks are those of the individual speakers and are not to be taken as representing the views of the Society.

The Proceedings of the Symposium of The John Bassett Moore Society of International Law are published annually.

The Virginia Journal of International Law is published 3 times a year at Clark Memorial Hall, University of Virginia School of Law, Charlottesville, Va. 22901. Subscriptions, orders for back numbers, correspondance with reference to the Journal, manuscripts, and books for review should be sent to the above address.

CONTENTS

THE WORLD POPULATION CRISIS: POLICY IMPLICATIONS AND THE ROLE OF LAW

FIRST SESSION

Friday, March 12, 1971, at 1:30 p.m.
Panel: The World Population Crisis: Policy Goals

SECOND SESSION

Friday, March 12, 1971, at 3:30 p.m.
Panel: The World Population Crisis: Institutions

THIRD SESSION
Friday, March 12, 1971, at 8 p.m.
Panel: The World Population Crisis:
Domestic and International Laws

FOURTH SESSION
Saturday, March 13, 1971, at 2:30 p.m.
Task Force Reports

SELECTED PAPERS

THE WORLD POPULATION CRISIS: AN INTRODUCTION

*By Mary Ellen Caldwell**

The world population crisis is a relatively new topic of domestic legal concern in the United States. Initiatives for decelerating the rates of population growth were taken over two decades ago by several foreign countries and, during the 1960's, by international organizations. India, for example, adopted an official anti-natalist population policy in 1951. By 1970, twenty-five of the less developed countries had announced a similar policy to cope with domestic overpopulation, and seventeen were officially supporting family planning activities. Unfortunately, however, "the remaining sixty sovereign nations had shown little interest in or support for family planning activities." [1]

In December 1962, the United Nations General Assembly concluded the first debate in its history devoted entirely to the subject of population and by 1968, a small population trust fund had been created in the population division of the United Nations Secretariat. With the aid of government contributions of over one and a half million dollars, the Secretariat recruited and trained a number of demographic advisers to work in Asia, Africa, and Latin America in order to help governments organize national programs. Since that time, international organizational interest and activity have expanded rapidly.

Throughout this twenty-year period of changing attitudes toward unlimited population growth, the United States

*Professor, Ohio State University School of Law; Chairman, Mershon Caribbean Seminar.

1. Dorothy Nortman, "Population and Family Planning Programs: A Factbook," Reports on Population/Family Planning, No. 2 (1970 Edition, July 1970), at 8. Nortman used three categories in her study: (1) nations with official anti-natalist policies and programs; (2) nations supporting family planning with no official policy; and (3) nations with no policy and little activity. Id. at 4.

government moved cautiously in the direction of forming and articulating an affirmative domestic population policy. It was not until March 1970, that Congress created a Commission on Population Growth and the American Future, charged with inquiry into five aspects of population growth in the United States:

> (1) the probable course of population growth, internal migration, and related demographic developments between now and the year 2000;
>
> (2) the resources in the public sector of the economy that will be required to deal with the anticipated growth in population;
>
> (3) the ways in which population growth may affect the activities of Federal, State and local government;
>
> (4) the impact of population growth on environmental pollution and on the depletion of natural resources; and
>
> (5) the various means appropriate to the ethical values and principles of this society by which our Nation can achieve a population level properly suited for its environmental, natural resources, and other needs. [2]

The Commission, thus limited to assessing domestic population trends and policies, is not likely to study the interrelations between domestic and foreign attitudes and practices in population matters. This is unfortunate indeed, since those interrelations may seriously affect the maintenance of world peace and security.

Despite the fact that population policy is generally regarded as a matter wholly within the domestic jurisdiction of a nation state, it is clear that overpopulation, however defined, may well give rise to international friction and disputes that endanger international

2. Population Growth and America's Future. An Interim Report prepared by the Commission of Population Growth and the American Future. Washington: Government Printing Office, 1971.

peace. For example, rural-urban migration within a country may severely impair that country's capacity to provide employment, housing, health and educational facilities, and to maintain civil order. As a consequence, incumbent political leaders could be forced to invoke external assistance to preserve peace and tranquility, thereby pushing a domestic issue onto the international stage.

On the other hand, some discouraged and dispossessed members of an overpopulated country may migrate, legally or illegally, as cheap labor or squatters, into less populous territories beyond national boundaries. If trouble develops between the "foreigners" and the nationals of the receiving state, and the emigrants are believed by their fellow nationals to be mistreated, the situation could lead to international friction which could culminate in breaches of international peace. If migrants occupy external territories containing valuable exploitable resources, their very presence may trigger the revival of the sending state's ancient border quarrels with the receiver state. History attests to the fact that sparsely populated border lands are attractive targets for overpopulated neighboring states.

In quite another context, if the economic conditions of one province of a country are more favorable than those in others, the most favored inhabitants may take "anticipatory self-protection" against the immigration of their fellow nationals by seceding, thereby raising the usual array of international questions concerning domestic jurisdiction and the rights of peoples to self-determination. These are but a few of the international war-peace implications of differential population pressures throughout the world.

Humanitarian concerns for the quality of life and environmental implications of technological development in areas of high population density have been explored at length elsewhere. This symposium is the first concrete evidence that international lawyers within the United States recognize the legal implications of population policies everywhere on earth.

Structured along a simplified, but well-defined, problem-solving model, the Symposium sought to identify policy goals, institutions, domestic and international law, and to design alternative policy proposals for various aspects of the so-called population crisis.

Panel I, Policy Goals, charged with the task of delineating

problems of population growth and suggesting means for dealing with them, evoked three different kinds of responses. They were a medical doctor's specifically technical concern for optimal means and opportunities for regulating fertility voluntarily at the individual level; an economist's cost-benefit analysis of programs intended to produce "instant" zero population growth (ZPG); and a population research director's identification of numerous social mechanisms that may be used in the pursuit of a given population policy.

Dr. Ravenholt grounded his plea for population policy in the three-fold formulation that would allow for maximum exercise of individual choice in a supply-demand market for means of birth control. Recognizing the objective need for fertility control in terms of social needs and maternal health, he recommended the creation of social and technological opportunities for individuals to respond to that need. Thus, one clear policy goal is the development of safe and effective preconceptive and postconceptive means that can be self-administered. Concomitant with the objective need for fertility regulation and the availability of suitable means is the policy objective of widespread education to alert entire populations of both the need and the availability of safe solutions. A third policy objective at the individual level is that of providing alternative fertility control means that are acceptable, ethically and aesthetically, among people who are disposed to engage in such regulation.

Professor Spengler, an economist, focused upon the advantages and disadvantages of stationary population growth – a goal seemingly sought by or for the peoples of a number of countries throughout the world, including our own. Among the advantages he enumerated are: (1) manpower and materials that would otherwise be absorbed by economic and population growth could be channeled into improving the quality of life of a stationary population; (2) presumably the only children ever born would be "wanted children;" (3) a stationary population would allow time to readjust the present maldistribution of living space; (4) pollution and degradation of the environment could be arrested or stabilized; and (5) opportunities for massive changes in life-styles would be enhanced.

On the debit side, however, a stationary population could produce the following social dislocations: (1) the population pyramid would be skewed to increase the relative number of older persons with a resulting age imbalance in power and economic institutions; (2) the labor force would be greatly narrowed and altered in terms of access, promotion, and mobility; (3) generally high levels of geographic and social mobility would be difficult to maintain; (4) the business sector would be forced to adjust production on a non-growth demand expectancy, and (5) individual expectations would no longer proceed on the basis of anticipated economic growth.

In balance, it appears that a stable population would be desirable, but difficult to attain. Therefore, says Professor Spengler, policy goals should include the development of penalty/reward systems to encourage a limitation on numbers, augmented by the development of legal norms that protect the right of every child to be born into a habitable, loving environment.

Dr. Freymann, Director of the Carolina Population Center, included in the definition of population policy all of the public decisions that directly or indirectly influence patterns of population growth and distribution. He focused on three levels of policy: the setting of overall goals, the identification of social mechanisms that can be tapped to achieve those goals, and finally the implementing of modalities required to achieve the overall goals. Among the most important tasks identified by Dr. Freymann are those of:

1) Promoting the availability of safe and efficient contraception and pregnancy termination;
2) Reducing nuptiality;
3) Supporting lower fertility in economic terms;
4) Supporting lower fertility in social-psychological terms;
5) Reducing social constraints on fertility reduction;
6) Reducing reproductive inefficiency, i.e. high infant mortality; and
7) Coercion.

The task of Panel II, Institutions, was to answer as many of the following questions as current data permit.

What agencies, public and private, at the national and international level, are concerned with the world population crisis?

John Keppel, of the United Nations, surveyed the work of the

UN system; the State Department's Philander Claxton reviewed United States governmental programs designed to assist the less developed countries; and political scientist Terry McCoy identified the principal organizations, external to developing countries, most of whose programs are anti-natalist in purpose and effect.

What are the agencies' policy goals?

Because the term "policy" is ambiguous, responses to this question were calculated to be varied, perhaps contradictory, and even nonresponsive. Lasswell and Kaplan [3] defined the term as "a course of action in relation to others" and have noted that the exercise of influence consists in "affecting the policies of others than the self." Without question, each of the external agencies canvassed by Professor McCoy and the other panelists seeks to influence the actions and behaviors of persons other than themselves. Implicit in many of their programs is the objective to slow the birth rate in countries perceived by the agencies as experiencing a current population crisis.

What are the agencies' strategies?

Political scientist Phyllis Piotrow suggested that any new policy, including a population policy, should be introduced not as a governmental goal, but as a sub-goal or tactic for the achievement of a goal already acknowledged and accepted. John Keppel's analysis of the manner in which the procedural formalities within international organizations tend to alert heads of state to the concern that others have about the "population problem" is one of the most informative contributions of the entire Symposium. Terry McCoy's functional typology suggested the wide variety of means, direct and indirect, used by existing agencies in the furtherance of their respective policy goals.

What resources are at the agencies' disposal?

On this question, too, Professor McCoy identified the principal sources of financial support available to the various organizations with which he dealt.

What impacts have existing institutions had on population change thus far?

The general consensus is that it is far too early to answer such a question. Programs are too new, strategies too varied, evaluation data too scarce to warrant even an unsophisticated guess. There is, however, rather clear evidence of increased official concern with

3. H. Lasswell & A. Kaplan, Power and Society (1950).

the issues involved in discussions of "population." Professor McCoy reported on the rapid increase in the number of nations that have adopted, within the last decade, expressly anti-natalist population policies. It is estimated by a United Nations study team that within the next five years, some twenty to twenty-five governments may decide to embark freshly on action programs. That more and more governments are receptive to the notion of taking population into account in their development programs indicates that influencers somewhere are beginning to affect official thinking about the role of population change at the national and international levels.

Are additional resources and institutions needed?

On this issue, the consensus was uniformly affirmative. It is apparent from Professor McCoy's charts, showing the distribution of agency activity and wide variations in agency functions, that many countries and many functions are almost untouched by the massive overall efforts thus far to affect local population change and/or policy.

What must be done?

Proposed answers to this question may be legion. The papers delivered here suggest that the highest priority must be given to the creation of a worldwide information center, charged with the responsibility of gathering, processing, and disseminating information about what is being done everywhere on earth with reference to the "world population crisis." Such an organization was recommended earlier this year in a report by a UN/UNESCO/WHO Mission proposing the establishment of a World Population Institute.

Closely related to the need for coordinated information is an enlarged capacity among all existing agencies for advisory and promotional activities. Expanded efforts along these lines would simply reinforce strategies that seem to have been most effective in the past, that of creating an awareness among opinion elites concerning the gravity of the population issue at both the local and international levels.

If, as appears likely, twenty to twenty-five governments embark upon population programs during the next few years, high priority should also be given to the task of training additional personnel needed in the establishment and operation of such programs.

In addition to the foregoing, there is a huge knowledge gap

that demands further research on every conceivable aspect of the population crisis.

Panel III, Domestic and International Laws, provided the legal framework for national action in the United States, in other countries, and in the international arena. Lawyers Harriet F. Pilpel and Johnson C. Montgomery (both of Panel II), law professor Cyril C. Means, Jr., and law student David Tundermann explored the domestic legal structure as it affects population and the supply-demand system of voluntary planned parenthood. They suggested areas of legal and administrative reform designed to ensure voluntariness and effectiveness of population deceleration policies in the United States.

Drs. Luke T. Lee and Thomas C. Lyons, Jr., dealt with the legal-policy responses of the less developed countries to their own internal population pressures. Dr. Lee analyzed in detail the legal structures of two types of developing societies in Africa: (1) those which have been forced to develop a number of interrelated laws designed to help reduce burgeoning populations, and (2) those which inherited pro-natalist laws from former colonial rulers and are beginning to adapt those laws to the demands of social and economic development, with an overriding interest in basic human rights.

Dr. Lyons' beautifully articulated analysis focused upon the various social and political impediments to change in traditionally pro-natalist societies. He believes that national pride, racial-cultural paranoia, elitism, fear of change, and other political-economic-ideological forces pose enormous difficulties for those who seek to implement anti-natalist policies in the countries most likely to suffer the greatest deprivations in this era of the "population explosion."

Law professor Ved P. Nanda set the stage for creative activity at the international level and brought the entire Symposium back to the point of original concern: what contributions can international lawyers make towards solving the world population crisis?

This Symposium volume speaks for itself. It is not a final statement; it is not a solution. It is a stimulating first step toward the development of a new field of international legal institutions and norms. Those who participated in these deliberations shared one common characteristic: an interest in the worldwide implications of national and international population policy. Otherwise, they were a diverse group of doctors, lawyers, economists, and political scientists; professors, researchers, and students; representatives from national and international governmental agencies, universities, and private organizations. Especially important were the inputs from foreign students, broadly representative of the developing countries in Africa, Asia, and Latin America.

The critical reader will find omissions and gaps in the overall work. Nevertheless, innovation is here and the law teachers among us are delighted that the law student members of the John Bassett Moore Society of International Law carried the primary responsibility for identifying an internationally relevant problem that gravely threatens the future of world order, and for convening an interdisciplinary task force charged with proposing alternative solutions to that problem. Whatever merit resides in the expert panelists' contributions, the community of international lawyers must rejoice that their numbers are being strengthened by young and vigorous talent. Clearly, this Symposium establishes the fact that differential rates of population growth and distribution, and diverse population policies are bona fide matters of international legal concern.

THE AMERICAN SOCIETY OF INTERNATIONAL LAW
REGIONAL MEETING
AND
THE JOHN BASSETT MOORE SOCIETY
OF INTERNATIONAL LAW SYMPOSIUM

The University of Virginia School of Law, Charlottesville, Va.

THE WORLD POPULATION CRISIS:
POLICY IMPLICATIONS AND THE ROLE OF LAW

First Session

Friday, March 12, 1971, at 1:30 p.m.

The World Population Crisis: Policy Goals

The session convened at 1:30 o'clock in East Hall of the University of Virginia School of Law, with Professor Mason Willrich of the University of Virginia School of Law moderating.

Professor Willrich. I will make just one observation at the outset of this Symposium, and that is that I believe we are beginning at the proper place. All too often there is a tendency to leap with abandon into the middle of an issue and thereby ignore the question of initial policy goals. This is particularly true when major social issues are to be discussed. So it is more than appropriate that, at this point, we begin our inquiry with a thorough treatment of the policy implications surrounding population growth and the attendant problems.

POLICY, TECHNOLOGY AND THE CONTROL OF FERTILITY

*By Dr. Reimert T. Ravenholt, M.D.**

It is delightful to see the rapid increase in participation on the part of the legal profession in working toward the solution of population problems. I personally feel that the legal world is responsible, in large measure, for many of the population-related problems, because the laws have been to this point in time remarkably pro-natalist in nature. Moreover, legal value systems of world-wide scope have been anti-communicative in terms of the dissemination of information dealing with sexual and contraceptive matters. Surely legal codes have had a profound impact upon the current population and the magnitude of the problem which we now face. The impact of the legal formulation can be observed when we consider countries where the laws have been more atuned to the problems of excess fertility. In Japan many of the leaders as well as the the Japanese people think that their birth rate is too low rather than too high. This phenomenon is to a considerable extent a function of the fact that they have been living under a different legal scheme with regard to the means of fertility control than has been the experience in the United States and in most of the other countries of the world.

But, of course, it takes quite a while to create a law; and it takes a longer period of time to create a notable change of direction. Laws have a great deal of inertia – that is, they are a type of inertial guidance system influencing the social realm, somewhat similar to the mechanism used in our modern aircraft. Laws depend upon this inertia of social opinion for their value. But it is an onerous thing when we suddenly come to the thoughtful realization that we are confronted by some difficult problems and that the old laws have no utility in that they impede the solution and therefore cannot render aid. This surely has been the case with respect to population-related problems. Therefore, we have had to struggle to change certain laws and policies which

*Director, Office of Population, Agency for International Development.

would lead toward a more optimal regulation of fertility in today's world.

The determinants of fertility control behavior can be divided into three main categories. It is useful to reduce one's understanding of what the principal determinants of fertility patterns are in terms of these three principal categories, each of which can, in turn, be sub-divided into many related sub-determinants. The first is the objective NEED for fertility control, which may, indeed, vary greatly from time to time and from place to place; the second is OPPORTUNITIES for controlling fertility; and the third is KNOWLEDGE of NEED and OPPORTUNITIES for controlling fertility.

There is a possible fourth determinant – namely the role of acceptability of control of fertility – but it is probably a sub-set of determinant three in that acceptability is the same as social knowledge. If a society knows that a change of fertility is needed, then a change of behavior needed to gain that end becomes more acceptable. We see this phenomenon at the present time. We are certainly living in a time when many activities are acceptable that were completely unacceptable 20 years ago. I think of the modern dormitory arrangements on many university campuses, which were strictly forbidden when I went to the University of Minnesota. But social policy has changed abruptly and much of the liberalization with respect to the dissemination of knowledge regarding reproduction, sex and control of fertility is the product of social need, and social understanding. There is a real need to change the attitudes and policies concerning the control of fertility.

There are two principal kinds of need for control of fertility. One is the social need – depending upon the balance between births and deaths in the world or in any specific country. The other is the need to control fertility among individuals from the maternal and child health point of view. There can be no doubt that the world has an enormous need for improved control of its fertility. As you may know, in the current year there are going to be approximately 133 million births in the world and only about 55 million deaths – a difference of about 78 million – which means that the world population is increasing about a million and a half this week or 210,000 daily or 9,000 this hour. So there results an acute imbalance between the rate of birth and rate of death. Unfortunately, this imbalance is most severe in those parts of the world where it can least be afforded – in the developing countries. The developed countries have lowered their fertility rates to the vicinity of one percent per annum growth rate, but the developing countries have failed to lower their rates of growth from the relatively high traditional levels. Yet, on the other hand, widespread public health programs and improved nutritional techniques have caused the death rates to fall precipitously. My particular concern is for this imbalance between births and deaths in the developing world which retards the economic and social development of many countries.

There is a fundamental equation which you might wish to consider, and that is – what I would refer to as the developmental equation – that: Resources/People = Well-being. It is a very simple equation, but I think it is very fundamental and powerful. And this is true whether one is speaking of food divided by the number of mouths for determining the quality of nutrition that they may have, or whether one is speaking of housing divided by the number of people and thereby determining the quality of housing that they have, or whether one is speaking of the number of classrooms or the number of teachers divided by the number of children who need to be educated. Whatever the application in the sphere of population, this basic equation still holds true – that the level of nutritional well-being, of housing well-being, of educational well-being can be determined by this equation.

For a long time it was assumed that the denominator of this equation, namely people, was a given – that it could not be modified by human intelligence, that we simply had to accept it and that we had to do the best we could to augment resource production. But we now realize that in societies without a tradition for the regulation of fertility we are simply spinning our developmental assistance wheels if we provide assistance which simply balloons the population without increasing the resources per capita. And so, our programs are directed now in a more balanced way toward developmental assistance in many countries. We know that we have to provide some assistance for fertility control as well as for improvement of agriculture and resource production. Yet we are using only five percent of the foreign assistance money for the implementation of population control programs. This is not a great deal, but on the other hand, it is a lot more than we once used. The funding of population control programs amounts to $100 million this year, and this goes to many intermediary groups who are also active in this field, some of whom are represented here.

So, on the one hand, the need for the control of fertility is determined by the imbalance in births and deaths. On the other hand, there is also a powerful need to control fertility for health purposes. This was the traditional need. This is what Margaret Sanger has emphasized: that women who are unable to control their fertility suffer severe ill health. In earlier times, there were enormous pressures upon family resources and upon the physical resources of women, and this socio-economic condition led to intolerable conditions in this country, even as it now does in many of the developing nations. The control of fertility is fundamentally linked to a woman's control or improvement of her health and well-being.

Traditionally there has been a strong family planning movement; individual voluntarism provided the impetus in the days when laws weighted against governments doing this. The private associations developed a very effective, or at least a considerably effective, activity. The private endeavors made considerable advances in this field but if fertility control is going to be effective there is a need for the application of tax dollars in support of improved family planning through official programs. And this is the phase we are now in. It has already been mentioned that one of the principal determinants of fertility control behavior is NEED. The second is OPPORTUNITIES for control of fertility. Table I (See Appendix) shows the implications of birth control technology for family planning programs. Determinations such as what can be done to improve fertility control and how to go about doing it and how much it would cost and what laws or policies are needed for effective control of fertility are integrally dependent upon the technology available for this purpose.

This simple table was formulated to demonstrate the five tiers of technology relating to population control. The first tier indicates the kind of means that existed for the control of fertility before 1870. These were simple means: abstinence, coitus interruptus, delayed marriage or non-marriage, crude vaginal barriers, douching and illegal abortion. With that kind of technology, the control of fertility was necessarily dependent upon education and strict policies or laws regulating sexual behavior. The world has seen effective control of fertility in certain countries by the application of such methodology. For example, in the case of Ireland there was a fundamental change in marriage patterns following the widespread potato famine of 1846. The resultant delay of marriage to the late twenties or even into the thirties effected considerable control over fertility. But in many other societies this method was not as effective. During the ensuing 90 years, there was a gradual evolution of technology to tier two. With the advent of vulcanized rubber, condoms and diaphragms became available, as well as vaginal chemicals, rhythm and surgical sterilization. The development of this technology led to a rather effective control of fertility in the developed countries and among the upper classes in virtually all countries. With tier-two technology, Europe and the United States were able to effect considerable control over fertility.

However, an exciting policy-linked development occurred during the 1960's with the addition of the oral contraceptives and intrauterine devices to the technology available for controlling fertility. For the first time, it became feasible to develop broad government-operated programs for the control of fertility in developing countries with low levels of literacy and development. We know from the programs which have been operated during the last decade that it *is* possible to make a very substantial impact on birthrates in developing countries, especially smaller developing countries, through intensive programs to make available tier-three technology and appropriate information. But still it takes, of course, a mighty delivery system, because we are now concerned with preventive action or foresight application of fertility control. And there are too many people who have difficulty exercising foresight in virtually any field, let alone in the field of fertility and reproduction!

Under the double onslaught of a social need for the control of population numbers and an improved understanding for the need for the control of fertility for health reasons, we are seeing a fundamental change of laws in the United States and in many other countries, particularly as they relate to the legal availability of abortion, a post-conceptive, or hindsight method of fertility control.

I would submit that when moving from a tier-three technology to tier-four technology – when a woman is able to invoke hindsight for the control of fertility – the matter of the degree of motivation and the extent of education needed for an effective fertility control program is vastly different than if only tier-three technology is being used. We are experiencing this shift right now – an abortion clinic recently opened on Eye Street in Washington, D.C., the Nation's Capital. A decade ago this would have been unthinkable. Now it is acceptable because society has recognized that there is a need for such a clinic. So there it is – right in the Nation's Capital – a method of fertility control which was simply not available in large-scale fashion to women a few years ago. And I would add that as far as getting to the bottom of some of our most difficult social-public health problems, the availability of a post-conceptive means of fertility control will have a more powerful impact toward that end than any other measure. It will now be possible to solve problems which we have never been able to solve before.

In the research field, we are rather excited by the rapidly developing evidence that we will be able, to a large extent, to leapfrog tier-four technology, which does depend upon a lot of clinics and clinical activity, to a fifth technological tier where there will be available "a non-toxic and completely effective substance which, when self-administered on a single occasion, would ensure the non-pregnant state of the completion of a monthly cycle."

We have had a remarkable breakthrough in the last year, a substance called *prostaglandins*, which we now know is effective for the induction of the menses at the moment that the woman may have missed her period, has been discovered. It is effective also for the induction of labor at term, if the woman wishes to deliver on Tuesday instead of on Sunday, or during the day instead of at night; this substance can clearly be used for that purpose. We also know that it should be possible for this to be self-administered because it can be applied vaginally and have the same effects as if it were administered intravenously. I see this as having enormous implications for the well-being of society throughout the world because finally the whole concept of the wanted child – is the child really wanted and will it be well cared for – will be served to an extent that we have not previously thought possible, because when women can obtain such a substance from drug stores, from non-clinical facilities as well as from clinical facilities, and they can induce the menses at any time, then a wanted child by definition will be one that the mother actually carries for six months without terminating the gestation. This means that there will be a high degree of commitment to the child's well-being, and it should have great implications as far as how well that child will be cared for and the kind of child and adult that it will become. (See Table 2).

So I can say in conclusion that there are many activities going on; most of the countries are either already actively engaged in development of family planning programs or now changing their policies as the prelude to such development of programs. The rush of events, the change of laws and policies, the rapid improvement in the availability of resources for family planning programs, and now the notable advances in technology all indicate that we will move rather rapidly during this decade toward solution of the most difficult population problems.

DEMOGRAPHIC ALTERNATIVES IN POPULATION POLICY

*By Joseph J. Spengler**

If the world were not so full of people, and most of them did not have to work so hard, there would be more time for them to get out and lie on the grass, and there would be more grass for them to lie on.

Don Marquis, in The Almost Perfect State

I shall dwell upon the advantage of a stationary population, or zero population growth, and point out some of the problems associated with it.

There is a wide degree of disparity in fertility in the world at present. Of course, this may be equalized with the methods of control which were emphasized by the previous speaker. There is also a very high degree of disparity in what I would call the concentration of economic or geographic power. Further reference will be made to this later on. In what follows I will examine, mainly from the vantage point of the United States, demographic alternatives, together with costs and advantages therewith associated, under three headings: 1) stationary versus growing

*Chairman, Department of Economics, Duke University.

population; 2) adjusting to the advent of a stationary population; and 3) stationary population in a politically and demographically disparate and divided world.

The advantages of a stationary population are at least five-fold. The first advantage is that the services of men and materials which would otherwise be absorbed by the population growth and equipping it with new instruments can instead be made available for improving the condition of the stationary population. In crude numbers, that advantage might work out something like this: if it costs about 4-5 percent of the national income to equip a one percent per year rate of growth of a stationary population, then a rate of growth of two or three percent, such as we have in many countries, will cost eight to twelve percent of the national income simply to offset the growth of the population. If we cut this growth down to zero, this 8-12 percent can be utilized to improve the condition of the existing population. Thus if average income is growing one percent per year, reducing population growth to zero permits an increase in the rate of growth per year of average income of something like one-half of one percent for each cut of one percent in the population growth rate down to zero.

There are several complementary aspects to this gain. When population is stationary, the trade cycle is diminished and there is less fluctuation in economic activity. Furthermore, the age composition of a population is more favorable to productivity when the population is stationary than if it is growing.

The second advantage consists of the elimination of unwanted births which is likely to be associated with having a stationary population; for then the family milieu for children will be very much improved over what it is today in many families.

Thirdly, given a stationary population, current maldistribution in space and accentuation of maldistribution in space can more easily be halted, thus allowing for greater control of the spacial problems.

The fourth advantage arises from the greater realizable control of pollution and the degradation of the environment. For, while pollution is associated with many factors other than the population crisis, population growth does accentuate it; hence if we bring population growth to a halt, we have at least gotten rid of that factor.

I think, fifthly, that if we have a stationary population, its advent may mean that the objectives of life can be somewhat re-oriented. We can reshape our life into a form more suitable to a Thoreau or a Whitman than the sort of life that we have today – one which doesn't have too much to commend it. This means, of course, that we have to bring the Madison Avenue Lorelei under control, since they are not disposed to contribute greatly to what I would call a Whitman-like existence.

Turning now to the problems associated with the advent of a stationary population – there is nothing in this world without its cost, as any economist should know. Of course, it is more interesting to stress the costs than the advantages. The first problem is associated with the increase in the relative number of older persons. In a stationary population, there would be something like 16 percent who are 65 years of age or older. Accordingly, if too much power were concentrated in the hands of the older people, we would have a gerontocracy. It would be in order, therefore, to set up institutional arrangements to distribute power more widely through the population, though, I hasten to add, not primarily to those under thirty!

In the kind of population that we envision, there will be more pensioners than we have today. These have been defrauded ever since the New Frontiers-men came to Washington in 1960, in that the purchasing power of the dollar has gone down 27 percent. Moreover, we can expect the purchasing power of the dollar to continue to go down until the forces generating inflation are brought under control. Our problem, therefore, is to protect the receivers of fixed income, particularly older people, from the erosion of purchasing power occasioned by policies currently pursued by our federal government.

There is also the matter of the right of older persons to employment. Employment is dominated to a considerable degree by corporation, trade-union, and governmental bureaucrats. Under these circumstances you have a good many people pushed out of work because it's more convenient for bureaucrats to set down a simple rule than it is to administer a policy rationally. It is necessary, therefore, to develop a system under which employment rights of older workers are protected. And I hasten to suggest to the law students that this is a very fine field to develop. Such a system of law and interpretation is now being worked out.

The second major problem is connected with promotion, moving forward in income and occupational status. Given a life expectancy of 42 years at age 20, by age 50 only about three out of four of those who entered the labor force at 20 will still be around. Death and morbidity thus create opportunities for advancement, much as in the Army, when a long war or a sickly season opens the ladder of opportunity to those who survive.

Suppose, however, that we have a life expectancy of 55 at age 20; then, by age 50, 96 percent of those entering the labor force at 20 are still alive. That makes it very hard for those down below to move up. What, in effect, will be needed, therefore, is a functional equivalent to a long war or a sickly season, or a rearrangement of the pattern of payment. We shall have to reduce the degree of correlation between age and remuneration.

A third problem is that of maintaining inter-industrial, inter-occupational, and inter-regional balance. This problem is not pronounced in a static, non-changing society. In a dynamic society, however, tastes are modified, changes in technology are usually unequally incident, and elasticity of demand varies widely. Accordingly, a good many people have to move around in order to keep occupations and industries in balance. Yet, in a stationary population, there are relatively fewer people to perform the balancing role.

Some people are migration prone. They prefer the place where they are not to the place where they are. They can thus bring about a balance. There will be a need, however, for more information than we now have in the form of job projections, on where employment is to be had, where opportunity is growing and where it is dying out. It will be necessary also to break down the barriers against mobility which presently exist, barriers associated with trade union arrangements, corporate arrangements and government policy. A high degree of mobility and flexibility will need to be attained.

The need for mobility will be accentuated by the fact that we are moving into a world in which there must be discretionary time and income. Of course, if people listen to advertisements and commit each extra dollar, or if everything breaks down in our age of malfunction, there will not be much discretionary time or income. But let us suppose that there is. Then people have money and time which isn't particularly committed and can be directed by whim. To cope with this volatility of expenditures we have to have a highly flexible society, otherwise the pattern of production will not be accommodated to the pattern of consumption. In a stationary population, however, it may, as suggested earlier, be harder to achieve flexibility and mobility.

There are two additional problems. One is objective in character; the other is subjective. By the objective one I mean this: in the past businessmen have always looked toward population growth instead of toward income growth to augment the demand for their goods and liquidate their mistakes. In a stationary population, this will not be the case, businessmen will have to count mainly upon the growth of per capita income. They will have to adjust their expectations and plan to conditions encountered in the stationary population.

The other problem is essentially subjective. Whereas in the past expectations of all sorts have been adjusted to the view that population will continue to grow, they will now have to be adjusted to non-growth. Initially, however, as it is realized that population isn't going to grow and that we are moving to a zero rate, many will be under considerable strain to accommodate their expectations to this new situation. If this is not done, if expectations are not in line with the underlying demographic situation, a good deal of frustration will be experienced and bad policy may result. The kind of problem involved is touched upon by Henry Adams in his *Education* and his interpretation of the 19th century and his comparison of it with what he projected for the rest of the present century.

Let me now turn to what it is like to be stationary in a growing world. Two kinds of pressures are accentuated. The pressure of numbers upon the Earth will increase. If we assign a value of one to the pressure of numbers, as of now, upon all of the resources of the earth which may or may not be utilized, then by the end of this century the pressure of numbers and consumption on the stock of resources will be about three times what it is now. By the year 2100 A.D. it could be about 45 times what it is now. We shall not therefore derive much relief from the relative reduction in our pressure of numbers on resources.

Indeed, the outcome could pose very real problems for countries like the United States and Japan, which are highly dependent on the import of raw materials and as well upon exports to supply the purchasing power to cover the importation of raw materials. This, of course, raises increasing problems associated with shipping. For example, it could be easy to destroy a large Japanese ship. Order should be at a premium, therefore, along with efforts to economize on the use of natural resources.

The other pressure is military in character, accentuated probably by the growing unrest and frustration in the developing world. Let us suppose that average income in the developed world is eight times as high as that of the underdeveloped world, instead of 12-15 times as high as international income data might suggest. Then, supposing the average income rises three percent per year in the underdeveloped countries, and one and a half in the developed countries, it would take 100 years or more before the underdeveloped world would have caught up; and during most of that period the absolute spread between the averages would have increased. Frustration is almost inevitable.

Most of the people in the underdeveloped world live in a few countries, of which only China, India, and Pakistan have any military power. Their military power is essentially defensive in character, however. The remaining three large underdeveloped countries – Indonesia, Brazil, and Nigeria – have neither great defensive nor offensive military power. Average incomes are small in these countries inasmuch as productivity is low. There is no danger to the developed world, therefore, unless its members engage in a third modern Pelopponesian War. The prospect of such should point the way to peace.

The underdeveloped world stands to gain tremendously from peace in the developed world. Thus, crude figures based on 1961 income data suggest that the GNP in the developed world runs about $877 billion, and in the underdeveloped world about $185 billion. Then, two and a half percent of industrialized-world income amounts to about 12 percent of the income of the underdeveloped world, enough to contribute greatly to the economic progress of the other world were it to be made available to them.

There is a tremendous advantage, therefore, to the underdeveloped world, providing that peace can be maintained in the developed world. Indeed, peace provides the underdeveloped world with the only opportunity it may have to progress economically.

Turning now to the matter of population optima, I shall not try to define optima for a country or a city or a region. It is essential, however, that every city, every region, and every country ask this question: Would further population be desirable? The metropolis of Denver asked this question and decided no, in that they have fixed a limit to how many people they are prepared to absorb.

Our problem then becomes one of building up a suitable reward and penalty system. Having decided on how many people we want, we must contrive penalty/reward systems to bring out the respective limitation of numbers. Today we lack such a system.

Also, we need action on the part of the legal profession. There is much talk about rights, but little study about the structure of rights. There is much discussion about the rights of people to procreate, but very little about the right of the child to be born into a satisfactory family milieu. Work on the structure of rights will help us fortify whatever incentive systems we have in order to keep the aggregate number of births at the right level and have them distributed among the elements comprising the population.

There is also the matter of population distribution to which I made reference earlier. We have not brought the distribution of our population over space under very effective control. And we pretend that it is subject to stochastic processes. Yet a stochastic process can be controlled as can any other. Attention needs to be given to bringing about an optimal distribution of our population, particularly if 75 to 100 million people come into the economy before the actual rate of population growth becomes zero.

Another point I would make is this: we may have to take steps to prevent the accumulation of unfavorable genes in the human gene pool, the primary resource of mankind for tomorrow. This pool is being increasingly fed by people who survive into the reproductive age and introduce genes which formerly did not get into the gene pool because in earlier time they perished before reaching that age.

I close, not with a conclusion, but with several implications of the line of argument advanced earlier. The population problem is extremely complicated; you cannot lift it out of the rest of the socio-economic structure in which it exists. Dealing with it entails dealing with the total structure and with all of the accompanying social dimensions. Unless we proceed this way, I doubt we can get very far.

THE DIMENSIONS OF POPULATION POLICY FORMULATION

*By Dr. Moye W. Freymann, M.D.**

This panel has been assigned the task of establishing the basic frameworks of thought which will enable further consideration of the policy approaches to population problems. I would like to add to the attempts of my predecessors to provide you with the dimensions of the problem by way of definition, categorization, and conceptual centralization.

The phenomenon of population policy is not an item that one can easily grapple with or master. The term implies all those kinds of public decisions which may influence, directly or indirectly, patterns of population growth and distribution. To understand the range of the possible effects of these policy decisions, and, just as importantly, the processes whereby policies are formulated and changed is not a simple accomplishment. In order to properly attack this broad subject, I think it important to break it down into manageable levels of population policy development. Beyond that, the policy implications and effects of each of these levels can be considered.

Overly simplified, the levels of population policy development can be observed in three steps. First, the setting of broad, all-encompassing goals. Second, the analysis of the "content" of the policy. At this level the policy refers to the social mechanisms which can be employed to achieve the basic goals. Third, the implementation level. This step implies other policy decisions about which sort of organizational moralities and officially sponsored activities can be utilized to alter the social mechanisms in order to achieve the desired goals.

In certain measure, the kinds of processes that are applied at the primary, goal-setting level have already been illuminated: studying present population trends; projecting future directions; analyzing possible alternatives; determining the costs of future alternatives – this costing process comprehends not only economic considerations but also dimensions of human ethical values which are highly prized and ought to be maintained;

*Director, Carolina Population Center, University of North Carolina.

considering the health aspects, which have, paradoxically, been grossly underestimated in many policy discussions; and lastly treating questions of resource conservation and management.

Having looked at these alternatives and costs, it is important to realize that there is a tremendous momentum built into any kind of a population system. This momentum of growth cannot be changed overnight; therefore some consideration ought to be given to the time dimension. All of these multi-faceted components enter into the goal-setting process, the principal thrust of which should be to establish the optimum direction of policy which will underpin the general goal. This somewhat complicated model of alternative balancing is that which must be invoked at the goal-setting level.

Now, the second level involves the use of social mechanisms to achieve policy goals. I would suggest to you that there are at least seventy types of categories that may be invoked to specifically alter the fertility component of population change. It is useful to bear in mind that these broad patterns are influenced not only by the fertility trends but also by the mortality migration trends of a given group. But let's focus on the fertility component. I think for ease of expression that this aspect of population policy ought to have a special name: demogenic policy – that aspect of policy that relates to the reproductive dimensions of the whole. Within this realm several categories can be individually treated as a social mechanism. The first would be promoting the availability of contraception and pregnancy termination.

The next one would involve reducing nuptiality. Another would involve economic support for smaller size families or lower fertility. Other social mechanisms would include reducing socio-psychological support, reducing the social constraints on reduction of fertility, reducing social supports for high fertility, and reducing reproductive inefficiency. The final one would be the use of outright coercion.

The fact remains that every known society has some sort of contraceptive or abortion methods which are indigenous to the society and have arisen through history. For example, we know that in India, and in many other countries, breast feeding is invoked purposely by women as a means of reducing the susceptibility to further pregnancy. And indeed, this helps to explain most of the sub-maximum fertility in India. But the fact is that most of these historically generated methods of contraception are very inefficient, as Dr. Ravenholt aptly pointed out. It naturally follows therefore that a good proportion of the world's people are demanding a supply of safe, efficient contraceptive methods and, in the case of failure of contraception, more convenient ways of terminating pregnancy. This is a world-wide phenomenon.

There is a great deal to be done in this realm, all of which is imbued with varying degrees of policy and legal implications.

With regard to reduction of nuptiality – the effective patterns of co-habitation of couples – we know historically that the reduction of birth rates in Western Europe, and now even in parts of Asia, is due not so much to the increased efficiency in contraception but to rising marriage age and the general reduction of the extent of nuptiality and marital patterns in the society.

We know that this is a terribly effective means of fertility control not only because it reduces the duration of co-habitation of individual couples but also because it increases the interval between generations; so that if you increase the inter-generation interval from 17 or 20 to 22 or 25 over a period of several generations, the total number of births even with the same specific fertility rates will be much lower. And there remain legal approaches to this mechanism, policy approaches too, which are virtually unexplored in much of the world.

Thirdly, with regard to the economic support mentioned, the tax structures, which in many cases are now inconsistent, may be pro-natalist in their design. Moreover, there may be other specific incentive systems that may act on this whole fertility generating system – things like educational allowances, rewards for later marriage and then in some several countries even incentives for the use and adoption of new contraceptive methods. Socio-psychological support would be an important category which exerts influence on public education by increasing knowledge. Such a mechanism results from policy decisions about what kind of information to make available and which conduits of information to use. Socially important channels and mechanisms such as schools, churches, and political parties have important roles to play at this level. In any event, the change of family size might be accelerated and facilitated by pervasive educational efforts.

The category of social reduction of supports for high fertility is aimed at a release from those cultural characteristics in the society which may have been established in previous years to support high fertility which was predicated upon the ultimate desirability of survival.

How does one break through these notions which support a high degree of fertility? This is another category where thought and action are needed before policies are implemented. Certainly a most important dimension of this is to change traditionally structured women's roles, to release women from a cultural mold that leaves child bearing as the only satisfying kind of career. Such an alteration would have implications for education, for employment, and for providing perhaps through policy decisions a guaranteed employment or a preferential employment for women in order to effect such a change.

There are yet other social/structural supports for high fertility in religion, in old age dependency on children for old age protection, and in benefits which may be approached through social policy measures in many societies.

The release from reproductive inefficiency refers to the sort of compensatory built-in high fertility that pervades, for example, societies where there is a high infant mortality rate or a high child mortality rate. In order to assure survival there habitually has been a compensatory over-production of children which results in a notable lag between the reduction of infant mortality and the reduction of fertility. But certainly all the evidence we have shows that reducing this mortality rate among children as rapidly as possible is a way to release people from the need for more births.

The sex of children is another dimension to which future research may give us better approaches, but now throughout the world the biologically random nature of sexual determination of newborns is quite inconsistent with social patterns. We have built into our society and many other societies a tendency for overcompensation in order to achieve at least one or two boys or one or two girls according to individual preferences; the result is a certain amount of excess fertility. Some day we may be able to release ourselves from it.

Finally, we come to the category of coercion, which has been the subject of a lot of debate and a lot of very diversionary debate since in most of the world almost none of these first six categories have been adequately approached. It carries with it all kinds of ethical traps, program-administrative traps, and biological dangers. I guess the overriding immediate problem with coercion is political; one epitomized by the comment that in most countries talking about these sorts of coercive measures would bring down the government faster than it would bring down the birthrates!

You have for your consideration problems of legal, ethical, political, administrative, and technical dimensions which are characteristic of each policy approach. None of these have been sufficiently considered, I think. We have been far too dependent on grasping at the straws of one approach or the other instead of looking at them realistically and seeing what sorts of combinations can be mustered to more efficiently manage our performance.

In conclusion, I think if we learn to think about these aspects of population goal-setting and implementation, we are learning an awfully lot about basic links between many different scientific disciplines. An important by-product of our concern with the population field will be the evolution of a much broader body of human scientific knowledge.

Also, I think dealing with this problem is forcing us to think more clearly and specifically about human values, about what we really want after all. We may come out of this era of concern over population with a more acceptable and relevant body of human ethics.

And finally, I think that if we can manage this very dramatic and basic problem on an international front, if we learn how to organize to meet it, then maybe we can organize to handle other overriding human problems between nations, and perhaps achieve the next great evolutionary challenge that we face of building the credibility of international law and of augmenting methods to keep peace among nations.

Discussion

Professor Willrich thanked the speakers for their remarks and observed that he felt that the panel had been invidiously discriminatory in that no mention was made of the rather fool-proof method of contraception – the vasectomy. Members of the audience were then called upon to make comments and ask questions based on the remarks of the panelists.

Mrs. Tinuade Oyekunle, of Nigeria, asked whether the

prostaglandins was now available and if so how effective is it and why has it not been made available to the less-developed nations?

Dr. Ravenholt indicated that the prostaglandins is now in the research and development phase. It is not presently available for general use or prescription. The various world-wide efforts to make available to all the best methods of contraception should not be slighted, but we presently are using the best methods known – the oral contraceptives, the IUD and sterilization. The prostaglandins represent the latest advancements of contraceptive technology. As has been noted, in 1968 there were no methods available for post-conceptive, self-administered fertility control. In the past three years, AID has directed most of its research and some $10 million toward acquiring an effective post-conceptive substance. As can be seen, this occurred in 1970. But is it effective, 100 per cent effective? Well, the best I can do is say that it has a potential for 100 percent effectiveness. Dr. Karim has reported that in his first trials of administering vaginally that it induced the menses in 11 out of 12 instances. Dr. Joseph Speidel, of the Office of Population, after a recent visit reported that Karim has extended the series to more than 100 without a single failure. The ultimate value of the prostaglandins is that it is a natural substance which occurs in the body. It may be the natural substance the body has always used for the regulation of uterine function, specifically for the induction of menses. So far as can be foreseen the matter of toxicity does not appear to be a major difficulty. When administered intravenously, it does cause some nausea, vomiting and diarrhea in a minor number of cases. But this may be viewed as a protective phenomenon in that it protects against administration of unduly large doses. But it does look as though it would be relatively non-toxic and that it will be completely effective and that it can be self-administered. It is currently being used for research purposes in a rapidly growing number of centers around the world. Initially some of the studies in 1970 were done in Uganda and in Sweden. Some work was done in this country. There has since been a rapid proliferation of research activities. When I was in Japan in October there were 10 Japanese universities using this in various kinds of research. But interestingly, in Japan while it was being used for blood pressure and induction of labor and various other things, there was a very noticeable sensitivity on the part of the Japanese to the use of prostaglandins for the control of fertility – which impressed me because it reinforced an impression I had received a year and a half before: that the Japanese society had become rather strongly pro-natalist in its orientation, and that they view prostaglandins as having rather profound implications for birthrates. This is another reason they have not made the oral contraceptive available in Japan; they do not wish to reduce the birthrate more. The effect of abortion has done this so powerfully. We are working with the Population Center at North Carolina developing a large, multinational study, a clinical trial which will go into effect this summer. The balance of this year will be devoted mainly to clinical trials in many cultures, and by the end of this year we hope to have the results. Next year there will no doubt be a substantial enlargement of availability of prostaglandins; licensing for prescription use I would view as not likely to occur before 1973.

Dr. Miriam Birdwhistell inquired as to whether there is an emphasis placed on making prostaglandins available on a non-prescription basis. She stated that the pill enjoys this status in some countries of the world. If prostaglandins were made available to all women in order to regulate their own menses, this would alleviate the social-psychological problem of destroying a fetus.

Dr. Ravenholt replied that he anticipated that it will ultimately become available as a non-prescription substance in most countries. There is no doubt that in the United States it will initially be sold by prescription; just as with the pill which is available without prescription in most countries of the world, but not in the United States. There is a hazard associated with the pill and yet it is very small as compared with the hazards of the pregnancy – even in this country. In the developing countries where the maternal mortality rates are often more than 500 deaths per 100,000 live births, the hazard from getting pregnant is hundreds of times greater than the hazard to life of a woman taking the pill for a year. There is a noticeable trend toward liberalization of availability of oral contraceptives in the developing countries – where it has made it available for distribution by nurse/midwives. In Brazil, which is more antagonistic to family planning than any country in the world, there is actually a very successful movement toward effective fertility control because the Brazilian women have been buying pills from the drugstore and using them in increasing numbers. There are now more than two and a half million women in Brazil using oral contraceptives, which is two-thirds of the rate of use in the United States. The key to it is to have something available that women really want.

Mr. Aklog Birara, of Ethiopia, stated that he had three questions. The first was that many authorities argue that the source of underdevelopment is not so much overpopulation but rather the ineffectiveness of governments to introduce rapid radical reform, and therefore is it possible to pick an issue and argue the point of whether large population increases are desirable? And the second question was that after we have argued that having a higher rate of population in fact increases the probability of capital accumulation for the developing countries, is it possible also to argue that the increase in population would in fact bring about capital accumulation in developing countries?

And the third question he asked dealt with the discriminatory availability of contraceptives and abortion. He further stated that population programs among the backward nations may carry undesirable political overtones if they are being urged by developed countries who are doing nothing in this regard. May not it be more practical in economic terms to prevent population growth in these developed nations, thus freeing more resources from the advanced consumption cycle?

Dr. Ravenholt answered by making the distinction between a problem of excess fertility and problems of governmental reform or equitable distribution of resources. Naturally, government reform and redistribution of resources should be carried forward, but excess fertility may or may not be applicable to the situation. The more basic problem is development. It is surprising that developed countries, virtually without exception have less births per thousand than do the developing nations – less than 20 per thousand as opposed to more than 30. Now, there has been a strong undercurrent, sometimes very much of an overcurrent, within our society and around the world with respect to who is doing what to whom. Who is trying to limit whose fertility? This is a very sensitive issue. The reason we have come so late to the whole matter of fertility control is that it has been an activity which was recognized intuitively as being somehow so fundamentally important for society that it should be approached very cautiously. But as far as the extension of effective fertility control around the world, I think we are on sound grounds when we view several fundamental principles: first, we are trying to extend to everyone the best means to control fertility as they see fit – no coercion is involved; second, we are exemplars in that we are proposing something that we are already doing. I think this is why the change in abortion laws in this country are so fundamentally important for our program in AID, because until this happened in New York and Washington we simply couldn't talk about this as an important contribution to the solution of the population problems of the world because we weren't doing it ourselves. Third, there is a remarkable universality among the various cultures of the world – particularly women. They want to control their fertility. There may be some divergence of opinion among politicians who seek this or that issue to which they can harness their political chariot, but the women of the world want effective control of fertility.

Dr. Spengler replied that he would answer no to all of the questions posed by Mr. Birara. When we look at the question of population growth, we also need to consider the various determinants of economic development; we cannot abstract the rate of population growth as the only cause of capital formulation – physical and educational capital. If we take all of these factors linked to capital per head figures, perhaps some countries could utilize more population. This may be the case for the eastern part of the Soviet Union, perhaps it would be true of Australia provided the Outback was usuable, but it would not be true for Latin America. Even though some increase in population could be utilized in some instances, it is better that it be achieved through a low rate of controlled population growth – particularly a rate which is associated with a low rate of mortality and natality which yields a more favorable age composition. Yet there are residual factors involved here which are not usually taken into account. Namely, it costs money to get from a smaller population to a larger one, and we are sometimes mistaken about the increases in returns. A low rate of population growth will cost less in the long run than a high rate. There is one other point: in some measure a larger population has certain advantages over a smaller one, for technological reasons. But there is an advantage to utilizing smaller scale technology which we feel can perform as effectively as large-scale technology, especially in light of the pressure of the population crisis. Generally speaking, then, most of the population growth has been disadvantageous; and where it is not disadvantageous, the major benefit is to be had from a slow rate of growth.

Dr. Freymann made two comments, one regarding the personal benefit dimension and the other concerning overall birth rates. Surveys in the United States indicate that people feel that 2.5 children per family is the ideal size. This 2.5 figure prevails among whites, among blacks, among the rich and among the poor. The only differential that has been found in any large percentage of the population is among the Catholics where it is about 20 per cent higher. But among the poor in the United States you get fertility rates which are about 50 percent higher than the well-to-do. We know that about 10 percent of the poor haven't any access to professional information or efficient contraceptive supplies. They simply do not have access to it. It is now a luxury of the well-to-do. The poor realize that this is a main reason for being kept in the cycle of poverty. It is also known that this excess fertility among the rich or the poor has a direct effect on the physical development of kids, and in their educational attainment and general health. You'd be surprised to hear that in the United States about 20 percent of the births are said to be unwanted by the parents. They actually say, "I really didn't want that child." If you apply medical indicators of optimal births, that is, not high risk births, there are about 30 percent of births in the United States that are medically contra-indicated, about 25 percent of brides in the United States are pregnant at the altar. But we have a problem of unwanted, excess births that's very profound. With respect to the growth aspect of the problem in the U.S., our yearly per capita consumption rate uses something like 40 percent of the natural resources in the world. We're consuming at a rate that causes the pressures to be exerted man for man by people in the United States on the environment, on resources that are 10 times what these pressures are in other parts of the world. Even though we are increasing maybe one percent per year that percentage produces much greater strain on our own environment and on ourselves than would be reflected in a straight statistic of one percent. We have a gross problem; and a very profound one is that of family welfare. The economists in the U.S. and the business leaders as well as the lawyers are all facing up to it for the first time.

Dr. Thomas H. Hunter of the University of Virginia School of Medicine complimented the panel on the manner in which they analyzed the complex problem of population policy. He then took issue with one of Dr. Ravenholt's statements concerning deaths, mortality, and decrease in mortality. The falling mortality in the developing world had been stated to be largely owing to public health measures and better nutrition. Dr. Hunter felt that this is an oversimplification, and that perhaps the falling mortality in these areas is much more attributable to less specific measures of general increase in socio-economic development than to medical causes. The public health measures are not to be incriminated as the one measure that has reduced mortality around the world. He further agreed with Dr. Freymann that controlled fertility is not accepted by most people around the world in the face of a very high infant mortality.

The session thereupon adjourned.

Second Session

Friday, March 12, 1971, at 3:30 p.m.

The World Population Crisis: Institutions

The session convened at 3:30 o'clock p.m. in East Hall of the Law School. Professor John Norton Moore of the University of Virginia School of Law presided. Before introducing the speakers Professor Moore made the following preliminary statement:

INSTITUTIONAL DECISION MAKING

Margaret Mead, in a conference on the population crisis about a year ago, indicated in her usual insightful manner that one of the things needed in the social sciences for dealing with problems is a "macroscope;" that the physical sciences have the microscope with which small problems are examined. But when it comes to an examination of the total picture, the total map of social issues, there is a notable lack of any kind of an instrument through which the scope of the problems can be specifically envisioned. At the present, the only available approximation we have is the tool of the human mind. This afternoon, our panel of distinguished guests will come as close as humanly possible to performing the functions of the futuristic "macroscope."

During this presentation, our panel will be primarily concerned with the institutions and the decision makers, how they come into being, and what role they play in formulating and implementing population policy. Also of import will be the recommendations for change in those institutions as perceived by the panelists for a more effective population control policy. In doing so, I suppose that it is appropriate to keep in mind that in terms of wide-spread realization of the seriousness of the population-related issues we have only recently begun to come to grips with the problem. In the pithy language of Pogo, it is only recently that we have met the enemy and realized that "they are us!"

THE DEVELOPMENT OF INSTITUTIONS TO MEET THE CRISIS

*By Philander P. Claxton, Jr.**

Even the beginning of an attack on the World Population Crisis requires the creation of a wide variety of institutions – and in fact a variety are being developed. It is my assignment to look at the needs for institutions and these early responses from the standpoint of a national government which has long had a major interest in assisting the efforts of developing nations toward economic development and social progress but has only recently become active in population matters.

Early Institution Building

We all know that the entry of the United States Government into the population field as an active agent was delayed long past the time when the population crisis had been recognized by many responsible leaders, including government officials. Fortunately, the process of building the institutions essential to the attack had already begun. The United Nations created its Population Commission as early as 1946 (ECOSOC Resolution 3 (III), Oct. 3, 1946). Several universities had established centers for population studies. The Rockefeller and Ford Foundations, the Population Council and the Pathfinder Fund were already at work. The International Planned Parenthood Federation was helping to establish and expand private family planning associations in dozens of countries.

Nevertheless, public, official U.S. Government attention was still lacking. In 1959, for example, a committee appointed by President Eisenhower to study the Mutual Security Program recommended that the U.S. assist countries asking our help to deal with their problems of rapid population growth. The President rejected the proposal as unsuitable for government interference. But the tide had begun to turn. President Kennedy in his 1961

*Special Assistant to the Secretary of State for Population Matters.

Message on Foreign Aid had recognized that in many parts of the world "population growth is already threatening to outpace economic growth." The time had come to initiate the process of United Nations leadership in recognizing, assessing and attacking the population explosion.

In December 1962, the U.S. joined 68 other nations in the General Assembly to adopt (69-0-27) a resolution recognizing that "economic and social development and population policies are closely interrelated" and that each government is responsible for its own policies in dealing with these problems. The resolution called on the Secretary-General to conduct an inquiry among UN members and specialized agencies on the problems created by this interrelationship. It also called on major UN bodies to study this interrelationship with particular reference to the needs of the developing countries to invest in health and educational facilities within the framework of their general development programs – in short, to consider what birth control programs they needed. A provision authorizing UN technical assistance to national programs dealing with population problems lost 34 to 34 with 32 abstentions, including the U.S., claiming that the authority already existed.

The Economic Commission for Asia and the Far East (ECAFE) in 1963 called on its own members "to take account of the urgent need to adopt a positive population policy related to their individual needs" and invited the UN and the specialized agencies to give governments, on request, technical assistance for statistics, research, experimentation and "action programmes related to population."

U.S. Government Interests and Policies

In January 1965, President Johnson brought the United States officially into the action with the declaration in his State of the Union Message that: "I will seek new ways to use our knowledge to help deal with the explosion in world population and the growing scarcity in world resources." This was an historic statement. The U.S. Agency for International Development immediately authorized its missions in developing countries to inform governments that it was prepared to help them with assistance, except contraceptives (that came in 1967), for family planning programs.

Meanwhile, the Executive Branch was under increasing pressure by the Congress to strengthen its own institutional framework for action in population matters at home and abroad. In mid-1966 the Executive created in the Department of Health, Education and Welfare an office of Deputy Assistant Secretary for Population and Family Planning and in the Department of State a Special Assistant to the Secretary for Population Matters. Shortly after, the AID moved to create a central Population Division and population staffs in each regional bureau.

State and AID rapidly began to create institutional arrangements in keeping with the scope and magnitude of the problems to be attacked. As a start, we tried to find out what the problem is and means. An analysis was made of the implications of population growth for the developing countries. It recognized, as President Johnson had earlier said, that "population growth now consumes about two-thirds of economic growth in the less developed world." It observed also, as the Senate Foreign Relations Committee said quite accurately: "Many of the benefits of aid are offset by population growth. Unless greater progress is made on control programs even massive aid will be relatively ineffective in raising living standards in many underdeveloped countries."

In short, the purpose of our substantial expenditures for foreign aid to improve the standards of living of the people of developing countries were being frustrated by run-away birth rates. In this context it became evident that for most developing countries their "population problem" was and is not just (in many cases not at all) a situation of high population density. It was and is the situation in which the rate of population growth is so high in relation to the ability of the country to provide goods and services for its people that improvement in the quality of life is slow or even non-existent. Moreover, our hopes that it might be possible to wipe out illiteracy and increase education were being dashed by the vast increase in numbers of children beyond the capacity of the developing countries to provide even elementary school educations. Studies also showed the existence of serious malnutrition and undernutrition among a large part of the world's population in many countries and serious dangers of massive famine in a few years. The escalating numbers of young people entering the labor force in country after country to find only unemployment, underemployment and bitter disappointment were becoming not only a growing mass of blighted hopes and lives but also the tinder for widespread social and political upheaval. With all of this, excessive fertility was providing untold misery of disease and death of young children, very high rates of illegal, inexpert abortions, orphaning of great numbers of children and general deprivation and hopelessness of parents.

In the light of this analysis, the U.S. Government determined to mobilize its own capacities and those of other competent institutions and to create new institutions as needed to help developing nations bring explosive population growth under control.

The institutions we have sought to strengthen or develop are necessarily appropriate to our policies and purposes. Several of these policies and purposes are basic and particularly relevant.

– Most fundamentally, we want to encourage and assist the leaders of developing countries suffering from the effects of high rates of population growth to recognize their situation and undertake effective programs to modernize birth rates just as death rates have been (and in many cases are still being) brought down to modern levels. It should not be necessary to add – but to leave no doubt I will emphasize – that each country will, of course, determine for itself what population/family planning policy it will follow.

– We believe that all couples are entitled as a matter of human right to the information and means necessary to determine responsibly the number and spacing of their children.

– We believe governments should assure that such information and means are available, not only in the interests of the individual family, but in the interests of mankind generally.

– We will assist population/family planning programs within a particular country only upon its request or where it has no objection.

– We will assist only those programs in which participation by individuals is voluntary.

– We believe the problem of bringing the population explosion under control is of such world-wide dimensions and appalling magnitude that the lead in attacking it should be taken on a worldwide basis by the agencies of the United Nations family and other international bodies.

– We will support such bodies in undertaking that leadership.

– We also believe the gravity of the problem requires the maximum attention by other donor nations and by those private organizations and foundations which can help effectively.

– Finally, although our internal population/family planning situation is radically different from that of most developing countries, it is important that we practice at home the principles we preach abroad.

These policies are directed toward our fundamental purpose of helping to improve the quality of life and enhance the human dignity of the individual citizen in the countries whose economic and social progress we are trying to aid. We do not consider population/family planning programs to be a substitute for assistance to development programs. We do consider them to be absolutely essential to the success of such development programs in most countries and to the attainment of many other important aspects of a better life for their peoples. At the same time, we do not condition our aid on the existence of any population policy or program.

U.S. Government Institution Building

The Congress in 1967 enacted Title X to the Foreign Assistance Act and stated its policy as follows:

It is the sense of the Congress that, while every nation is and should be free to determine its own policies and procedures with respect to problems of population growth and family planning within its own boundaries, nevertheless, voluntary family planning programs to provide individual couples with the knowledge and medical facilities to plan their family size in accordance with their own moral convictions and the latest medical information, can make a substantial contribution to improve health, family stability, greater individual opportunity, economic development, a sufficiency of food, and a higher standard of living.

– AID in 1966 had only 11 people in Washington and the field working full time on population matters – compared to 1100 working on development of agriculture. This number has now risen to an authorization of 154 full-time population officers with staff in a Population Division, each regional bureau and a full- or part-time population officer in each mission abroad – in certain key missions, a staff of several. AID provides bilateral assistance to

31 countries and many international and private agencies.

– USIA provides information on population growth, its implications for economic development and social progress, including maternal and child health and a better quality of life.

– Peace Corps volunteers in several countries are assisting local people in family planning programs.

The resources of other government agencies have also been mobilized, particularly the capacity of the Bureau of the Census to assist developing countries with demographic surveys and training in census work and the technical skills of the health and education experts of the Department of Health, Education and Welfare and the research program of its Center for Population Research.

Moving outward, the Government has sought to encourage and, as needed, support the work of private foundations, agencies and other institutions. AID provides institutional grant support to several established university population centers and has provided funds to the East-West Center in Hawaii to create a needed new Population Institute for the Asian region. AID also provides substantial support to the International Planned Parenthood Federation which, with funds from other contributors, helps to sustain private family planning associations in over two score developing countries. AID also provides grants or has contracts with about 80 other private organizations, each undertaking a needed, special role.

To help bring the capacities of international organizations to bear on the population problem, the U.S. has supplied the Colombo Plan Organization with a full-time population expert working particularly on population education. The U.S. has joined with several other countries to establish and support in the Development Center of the Organization for Economic Cooperation and Development a group of population specialists who, among other things, help the OECD member nations collaborate with other major agencies and organizations in population activities. The U.S. has encouraged the development in the Organization of American States of what is still a very limited population activity, quite inadequate for the needs of the region and the importance of the OAS. The U.S. has also supported in the Middle East the initiative of the Central Treaty Organization for an expanding program of consultation on population/family planning matters among member governments.

United Nations Institutions

The apex of the institutional effort has, of course, been the United Nations and its related bodies. Continuing the gradual development of UN doctrine, the Economic and Social Council in 1965 requested the Secretary-General to provide "advisory services and training on action programmes in the field of population" to requesting governments. In the same year the U.S. moved with others in the World Health Assembly to request the World Health Organization to undertake studies on fertility control and the health aspects of population dynamics and to provide "technical advice on the health aspects of human reproduction" but "not provide operational activities."

In order to assure the availability within the UN family of funds for population programs, Secretary-General U Thant in 1967 created the Population Trust Fund – later transferred to the UN Development Programme as the Fund for Population Activities. The Fund was intended to make money available to UN agencies, governments and private organizations for population/family planning programs outside regular budgets. To be effective, the Fund needed a staff of field workers to help national governments put their needs for assistance for population/family planning programs in a form suitable for consideration by the Fund. The U.S. made an initial contribution of $500,000 to create the needed institution of Population Program Officers stationed around the world. With this beginning, the Fund solicited contributions from UN Members and began to receive them. The General Assembly in December 1966 called upon all UN bodies "to assist, when requested, in further developing and strengthening national and regional facilities for training, research, information and advising services in the field of population."

With the background of ECOSOC and General Assembly approval and with special funds available for population activities, the governing bodies of all UN agencies with a potential role in attacking the population problem have adopted the necessary resolutions to authorize actions by it: the World Health Organization to provide family planning services and training; the Children's Fund to assist with materiel; the UN Educational,

Scientific and Cultural Organization to provide help with education, mass communications and social services; the Food and Agriculture Organization to develop programs of Better Family Living through its program of home economics, agricultural extension and community development; the International Labor Organization to develop information and education for labor and management.

In addition, the UN Commission on the Status of Women adopted resolutions (1965, 1966 and 1968) welcoming the increasing role of the UN in providing assistance in family planning and calling for studies of the status of women and family planning. The second International Conference on Human Rights in Tehran (April-May 1968) adopted a resolution that "couples have a basic human right to decide freely and responsibly on the number and spacing of their children and a right to adequate education and information in this respect." The Declaration on Social Development drafted in 1968 by the UN Commission on Social Development and adopted by the General Assembly in December 1969 calls for "the provision to families of the knowledge and means necessary to enable them to exercise their right to determine freely and responsibly the number and spacing of their children."

The Economic and Social Council in a series of resolutions has urged (1967) all organizations in the UN system to render more effective services in the population filed and has called (1968) "attention to the interrelation between population dynamics and economic and social growth with respect to the Second Development Decade."

The Population Commission, ECAFE, the UN's Expert Committee on Development Planning and others urged the necessity of recognizing in the basic Strategy Paper for the UNDD II the need for smaller families as "among the essential aspects of development strategy." Nevertheless, the determined opposition of a very small number of countries in the Preparatory Committee, where a consensus was required, precluded even consideration of the recommended language. As a result, the Strategy Paper includes only a vague statement on this basic element of economic development. For whatever value it might otherwise have, the paper is gravely deficient in a vital sector.

The Population Commission and the General Assembly also

recommended and the General Assembly approved a Population Year for 1974, including a Third UN World Population Conference.

The doctrinal framework for action in the field of population/family planning now exists for all UN agencies. The immediate task is to create the determination, establish appropriate internal and field organizations, recruit qualified personnel and generate action itself. The Population Division of the UN itself has for several years been providing indispensible leadership. The work of the UN Fund for these purposes is well under way. Nevertheless, with an increase in commitments to it from less than $5,000,000 before 1970, up to $15,000,000 for 1970 and a probable $25,000,000 or more for 1971, the Fund will need to increase its staff and scope of action substantially while managing a rapidly increasing load of requests. WHO and the Children's Fund are well advanced with the necessary personnel, training and programming. ILO has made a good beginning. UNESCO and FAO, both responsible for vital sectors, are regrettably lagging behind.

The World Bank has recently undertaken a major role of leadership in analyzing the burden which rapid population growth is putting on development for many countries. The Bank has also recently made two loans, one to Jamaica, the other to Tunisia, to construct maternity and related facilities to extend family planning services, particularly into rural areas where facilities do not exist.

The Commission on International Development (Pearson Commission), appointed by the World Bank to examine and report on the requirements for the successful economic development and social progress of the developing nations, said of the population explosion: "No other phenomenon casts a darker shadow over the prospects for international development than the staggering growth of population."

It may be obvious, but nevertheless should not be left unsaid, that no matter how complete an institutional establishment may be created at the top, little will be accomplished unless necessary and effective institutions are created at the regional and local country levels.

It is important that the Economic Commission for Asia and the Far East (ECAFE) and the Economic Commission for Africa have both established special units for population matters and are beginning to undertake major program action. The U.S. has assisted both Commissions with substantial grants through the UN Fund. Only the Economic Commission for Latin America (ECLA), in the region suffering most heavily from very high rates of population growth, has failed to prepare itself for or undertake any significant role.

A unique institution has recently been created by several governments in Southeast Asia – an Intergovernmental Coordinating Committee on Family and Population Planning in Southeast Asia, with its own small secretariat at Kuala Lumpur, to coordinate information, ideas and possibilities for joint action for their several national programs to slow population growth.

Another unique institution has developed from an informal meeting at Bellagio, Italy, of the heads of aid organizations of donor governments, of principal UN bodies and of several major private organizations. The purpose of this group is to identify the more difficult obstacles to the success of population programs and then develop ideas and coordinate action to attack them. The group has a steering committee headed by Mr. Rafael Salas, Executive Director of the UNFPA.

The UN has also sponsored or assisted regional centers for population research and training at Chembur in India, in Cairo, and in Santiago, Chile. The UN with its Economic Commission for Africa is now establishing a Demographic Center for Anglophone countries in association with the University of Ghana and a similar Demographic Center for Francophone countries at Yaounde, Cameroon.

We believe it is important that broadly interdisciplinary population education and training centers should be created in other regions and in at least a half-dozen large countries and several smaller ones with population programs. The U.S. is now helping the University of Ghana establish such a center and considering possibilities in other areas.

Ultimately, of course, the success of the world's efforts to bring the population explosion under control will depend on the effectiveness of institutions developed in each individual country to help the individual citizens control their fertility – and the actions of those individuals. The national institutions which must provide positive support include, among others, legal, administrative, health services, public information, educational, tax structures and old age pensions. Major changes may be necessary in such institutional and cultural patterns as the age of marriage, the extended family, attitudes toward childbearing and family size, governmental and private child support, abortion, rights of women to jobs and property, land ownership, attitudes of males toward fertility control, and many others. The evolution of attitudes within such existing institutions as the church and organized medicine will be important.

There will be many additional changes among the institutions of the donor nations. Here in the United States, the President has already proposed to the Congress that the present Agency for International Development be succeeded by several agencies with more limited responsibilities. The administration of population programs would be transferred to a proposed International Development Institute. Happily, the proposals for the new IDI place population programs first on the list of activities it is to undertake. Abroad, we should look for an increase in the number of countries providing assistance to population/family planning programs and to the amounts of their contributions for such purposes and to the variety of assistance provided by them.

Yet we are still only dimly aware of the size and complexity of the effort needed to counter the population explosion. For this reason, President Nixon has asked the UN Fund to make a study of the scope and implications of the population growth problem and of what together we must really do to bring it under control before nature restores the balance with the traditional means of starvation, pestilence and violence.

We are looking forward to this study for guidance because we know that, despite the remarkable institutional developments of a very few years, we should not suffer any illusions that we have done more than begin the monumental task of bringing birth rates again in line with death rates – but at a modern and humane level. When together we have a clearer idea of what we must do, there is reason to expect that the world as a whole will rapidly increase the breadth and variety of the effort given to this task.

We cannot blind ourselves to the advice of our National Academy of Sciences: "Either the birth rate of the world must come down or the death rate must go back up." This inhumane alternative to a massive reduction in birth rates is too terrible to contemplate – or to entertain seriously. The only humane course for nations and for individuals is to act with resolution and speed, using the means science makes available and, constantly respecting individual rights and human dignity, to help modernize birth rates as death rates have been and are modernized.

THE PROCESS OF INSTITUTIONAL POLICY FORMATION

*By Phyllis T. Piotrow**

There is always a certain temptation on the part of women in this field, to which I usually succumb, to regard the population problem as one that could be very easily resolved if we removed a great many of the restrictions that have been imposed by professionals of various sorts, the lawyers and doctors. These restrictions limit the ability of women to do what I think most women want to do: retain some degree of personal control over their own fertility. Therefore, a woman's voice in this respect does have a particular significance.

I am going to discuss very briefly a pattern that one might use for looking at the development of government policies in the field of population. One could use it equally well to look at the development of policy for environment, or for medical care, or for defense policy or any other area, but I think applying the pattern to population as well as looking at these other areas helps to bring the subject into focus with the various aspects of government policy. This approach was developed by Samuel Huntington in his classic book *The Common Defense,* which discusses the development of new defense policies.

First, the introduction of any new policy, such as a population policy, into government proceeds usually not by introducing a new objective into government, such as a goal for population control, but rather by attaching the idea of population as a sub-goal, as a tactic, as a means of achieving some other goal that is already acknowledged as a valid government objective.

*Population Crisis Committee

The Relevance of Policy

In the course of the development of governmental policy in the United States, which Mr. Claxton has outlined, I would say that the population problem came into the purview of government policymakers as a sub-goal, a sort of tactic, to achieve the basic strategy of economic development. I would argue rather strongly that it was not as a means of achieving better health. When you come right down to it, the people whose health are affected by lack of birth control tend to be vulnerable, weak, helpless, rather negligent women. I submit that legislative bodies of the world do not go very far out of their way to look after the health of women under those circumstances. It was only when population was considered in terms of how relevant it is or was or continues to be to the goal of economic development that the United States government became involved. Similarly, other governments take up a policy when it is a means or is relevant to an existing and accepted government objective.

The United States, as a government, began providing birth control assistance overseas before it was providing birth control assistance as a government within the United States, because it perceived economic development problems, in India, for example, as being more difficult than those in the United States. But I would also say that we learned from our foreign aid program. We learned that if poverty in India is caused by overpopulation, it is also possible that in the United States poverty may be caused, and certainly aggravated, by overly large families in individual cases.

The reason why one finds the United States Government developing family planning programs more consistently, more easily, and I think in many ways better in AID and under the aegis of the Office of Economic Opportunity than has been the case so far with the HEW program is because it was much easier for government policymakers to perceive family planning as relevant to the war on world hunger and the war on poverty; family planning is a good tactic to fight poverty. It is a great deal more difficult to show how family planning is that much better for the health of everyone concerned. It can be done, but it is difficult, and I think the doctors have a responsibility here that they haven't quite yet fulfilled. That argument is still weak in many respects. In the United States the policy came about through an appreciation of the relevance of family planning to economic development, or to individual economic opportunity, not through a concern for health.

Policy Feasibility

Now, after the question of relevance, the next issue that has to be considered before a government policy is undertaken is feasibility. We might think of a population policy that would consist of shipping people off to the planets, but there's no point in it, because it simply isn't feasible. We could think of putting anti-fertility drugs in the water supply, but it isn't feasible either. These things are not technically feasible, so we do not think of government policy in those terms.

However, it became technically feasible to think of government family-planning policies with the development of the Pill and the IUD. That was in the 1960's. The question of technical feasibility is generally determined by specialists, experts, professionals, scientists, who work in the corner of some laboratory inventing something that will solve the technical problem.

The other aspect of feasibility that must be established before a government policy is embraced is political feasibility. In the United States, it did not seem politically feasible to do anything about birth control until the 1960's because of the extent of opposition by the Catholic Church. But within the Catholic Church, the election of Pope John XXIII, the Ecumenical Councils, as well as the pressure for more liberal public policies in the United States from Planned Parenthood and other organizations, forced a change in the position of the Catholic Church. The first step in this change was when Catholics began to say publicly: "We think birth control is wrong, but if Protestants and Jews want these wicked things, then we won't try and stop them. We'll go to Heaven and they won't; that's their business." This argument is known as "the pluralistic society" argument – we go our way, they go theirs. This change in thinking made it possible for many state laws to be changed. Presumably, the Catholic priests still expected everyone to be damned if they used birth control, but they no longer worried as much about saving non-Catholic souls.

The next step came, I think, when Catholic leaders realized that most Catholics didn't believe they were being damned by using birth control either. As the problem developed within the Church, the leaders of the Church and the ordinary Catholic laymen were at loggerheads on this issue. Soon it became evident in the American political arena that the principal opponent of birth control, the Catholic Church, was itself hopelessly divided on the issue. In fact, between 1962, when the first hint of a Papal study commission began to come out, until 1968, the Catholic Church was really saying, again and again: "We're studying this question; we have this commission, we have that commission, we can't make up our minds; we're still studying it."

That six-year period of indecision, when Catholic commissions at various levels were studying the question, contributed tremendously to the political feasibility of taking up this subject. We in the population field congratulate ourselves on what a good job we have done in changing policy so rapidly but much of the change was only very indirectly our doing. Aside from the fact that the population continued to grow, and therefore, objectively, the problem continued to mount, the assessments that were going on within the Catholic Church had a great deal to do with establishing the political feasibility of government policy.

Policy Priorities

The third step, after feasibility, is a question of priorities. You can agree that something is relevant and feasible, but there are still perhaps twenty other things that you would rather do instead because they are more important, or because they will achieve the same purpose.

For a long time, for instance, in AID it would be said: "Well, yes, we think population is very important, and we could do something more about it, but we think it's more important to build schools, or it's more important to build cement factories, or dams, or fertilizer factories." Population is important, but when it came to allocating the money – and there's never enough money to go around – it was always decided that population didn't have as high a priority as these other questions.

The matter of priorities – of all the programs that are competing for personnel, resources, and funding which are the most important – is a question that always has to be decided from the top. Basically, decisions on priority are power decisions. They have to be made by people who have power. Sometimes the President will say, "This program is very important; therefore this is where the money will be spent." In the case of the population programs, the President and the Executive Agencies did not say that. It was the Congress, having the power to allocate the money, that said: "We think this program deserves priority." They demonstrated their power by earmarking the money, at least for their foreign program, in such a way that it had to be spent for population. There was no other power in the government that could countermand that decision due to the manner in which it was formulated.

Priority decisions are always difficult decisions. Up until the question of priority was considered, doctors, sociologists, demographers, economists, and public administrators could all agree that the subject was important. But when it came to the issue of deciding priority, they became rivals. Somebody's ox is going to be gored, because there is never enough to go around. What one person or program gets, someone else is not going to get.

So the priority decisions are critical decisions. They frequently split people, forces, and groups. Those who started out as allies on an issue find themselves suddenly fighting with each other for the money. This has been, I would say, one of the biggest troubles in the U.S. domestic arena; there are so many different groups that all feel that they are entitled to a certain share in the domestic HEW program that when you try to redivide that pie, by giving more to population and less to tuberculosis, or less to crippled children, or less to the deaf, or less to the blind, you find that you've made a tremendous number of enemies who are quite prepared to steal the population money away from you if they can.

The most painless way to make priority decisions is always to add more money, rather than to take it away from those who already have it. In the AID program the Title X that provided population money did add something, because it allowed loans to be used as grants. But in any program, in any policy, when it comes to deciding priority, somebody is going to get hurt somewhere along the way.

Question of Timeliness

Then the fourth and last step in this policymaking pattern, would be the question of timing. You can say: "Yes, it's relevant. Yes, it's feasible." And you can make a lot of speeches saying it's very important. But you can always qualify them by saying: "Yes, population is very important, but this particular year it's more important to build schools, or that it's more important to save ten medical schools from bankruptcy, or that there is some other crisis." The population crisis, by its very nature, is a chronic not an acute condition, to use medical terms.

Every time a population problem seems to develop you can always say it is something else. For instance, suppose that in one year you have six or seven million births, you could say: That's not a population crisis; it's an obstetrical crisis. Then five years later, one could add, "It is not a population crisis; it's a kindergarten crisis." Or it's an educational crisis, and then fifteen years later it's an employment crisis. Whatever difficulties a population crisis makes can always in some way be attributed to something else.

Individually in each instance, in all fairness, that is strictly true. But if you look at the whole conglomerate of what the population crisis involves, it is very difficult to envision that we could solve every one of those ten or fifteen other crises as they come along, without in fact getting to the crux of it – the population crisis.

But one great difficulty in establishing population policy is this question of time. How do you make it sufficiently urgent? Huntington suggests that in the Defense Department, in the field of weapons development, the ideal kind of crisis is to be able to say that in three or four years the Russians will have developed a certain weapon. This is the perfect argument for immediately appropriating a large sum of money for the United States to develop the weapon, whatever it might be. It is close enough to be a threat but not so close that our reaction will be hopeless.

It is hard to get this kind of a trigger event in population policy. The trigger event that started the United States Government moving in the population field happened to be the rather irrelevant fact of the failure of two successive monsoons in

India, a phenomenon which had not occurred for many centuries. In the fall of 1965, and again in the fall of 1966, the monsoons failed in India. The resultant publicity, concern, and discussion about the world food crisis were the principal factors that encouraged the U.S. Congress, in the year 1967, to decide that the population problem did deserve this high priority. The timing was such that something had to be done immediately. This is what I would call the trigger event; it certainly moved the first stage of United States Government population policy to the commitment of real funds for a regular program.

It was no coincidence that in the foreign aid agency, where the population program really started, that it was part of something called the War on Hunger. Now, how could you be against a war on hunger? No one could oppose the war on hunger. The professionals in any field often object when others try to publiize or even exploit the occurrence of a trigger event to promote government action. The demographers will say it isn't really a food crisis because we can produce Miracle Wheat in five years. When you get an environment crisis, you still have the demographers blaming the crisis on another cause. There is, therefore, a professional objection to using a trigger event to move government policy ahead. Yet without trigger events, particularly in a field like population, it becomes very difficult to move government policy at all.

Without going into any more ramifications, I would conclude that a basic issue when it comes to setting government policy tends to be a question of time versus resources. If the crisis is immediate, and is very urgent, as for instance if the Russians suddenly developed something more terrible than the hydrogen bomb, then the timing factor would overcome everything else. We would immediately expend a maximum amount of resources to alleviate the pressure.

When any new program comes along, the opponents of it will always argue that the timing is not that urgent, that it doesn't require that many resources, and that this can be put off and studied for another ten or fifteen years. They insinuate that the answers will be better then than now.

The proponents, those urging action, will almost always be stressing the timing element, the need to do something immediately, because if something is not done right now about this particular crisis, then the result is going to be so much more terrible that all the other programs are going to be adversely affected by the results of inaction at this point.

I will conclude by making a suggestion that contradicts in small measure what I said before. I started by saying that population policy is developed only as a means, as a sub-goal, or a tactic, rather than a comprehensive strategy. Perhaps we need now to go further than that.

One of the simplest economic concepts is that of scarcity. The value of a commodity is measurably increased as it becomes scarcer. In other words, we use slate and gravel for paving streets because it is in ample supply; we place diamonds in fancy settings as jewelry because they are scarce. Diamonds would undoubtedly make fine paving, because they are very hard, but because they are also scarce, we do not use diamonds for paving streets.

The real problem that we face in the population crisis is that as the number of human beings increases, the value of each individual human being, whether one admits it or not, does tend to decrease, especially within one's conception of human dignity and human worth. When we look at the very real fact that value today is often determined by supply, the greatest danger is that by increasing the supply of human beings, we are in fact very definitely decreasing the value of each individual. I would hate to think that the day might come, even figuratively, when people would cease to be valued, like diamonds, and be used instead like slate and gravel to pave the streets.

Even now we are increasing the number of restrictions that have to be placed on each individual so that he can get along with other individuals in a more crowded environment. In every respect, whatever we may say about human values and human dignity in general, we are downgrading the freedom and the opportunity that any one individual in the conglomerate can enjoy when that conglomerate becomes too large.

Therefore, I would suggest that we might begin to start thinking of population policy, not as it has developed in the past as a means to achieve some other end. We really need to start exploring the ways in which population policy may become more of an end in itself. If we permit population to grow to greater levels, the measures that we will have to take to organize our society to deal with very large populations will perforce be measures that will treat human beings as a far cheaper commodity, possessing a far lower intrinsic value than I think is the case where there are smaller numbers. The relative value of scarcity, the appreciation of what individual human beings are and can produce, must not be destroyed by massive reproduction and overpopulation. We want to continue to look upon people as valuable resources rather than as a surplus of one kind or another.

THE TAXONOMY OF EXTERNAL ASSISTANCE ORGANIZATIONS

*By Terry McCoy**

I am also interested in the question of how governments react to problems but at a slightly different level. Specifically, what interests me is the impact of international population programs on the population policies of developing nations. Clearly, the discovery of the "population explosion" has produced a "secondary explosion" – the rapid proliferation of assistance from international agencies, private foundations, and developed countries for the control of demographic growth in developing countries. What have been the effects of this assistance on demographic change in developing areas?

Here I shall summarize some research which represents a preliminary attempt to answer this question.

Specifically, I am concerned with the impact of international population programs on population policy – not upon the results of these policies, but upon the policies themselves of the less-developed countries, the assumption being that national government policy in the developing countries is of some relevance to future population growth and change. What governments do is important.

Now, I should perhaps begin by defining what I mean by "national population policy." Since much to my surprise, no one has attempted to define it, I will offer a definition that will include not only the status of public programs but also governmental attitudes, what is the atmosphere in country X, the official attitude regarding family planning, population size and

*Professor, Ohio State University; Mershon Caribbean Seminar.

population growth. It also encompasses private population family planning activities permitted by the government.

There are three broad alternatives, according to this definition; first, the government can be officially anti-natalist; "officially" means to publicly support family planning and seek to limit population growth. The opposite of this is an officially pro-natalist policy – against family planning and encouraging population growth. In between is where most governments in fact fall. There are governments with no official policy, no systematic public declarations about the population issue, but there are indications that a government supports or does not support family planning and population programs.

What impact, if any, does the whole complex of international organizations that have some kind of population assistance have on the population policies of less-developed countries? Perhaps I can illustrate this by a model of the policy process. (See Figure 1. "Policy Process of a Typical LDC").

The solid box refers to official decision-makers in any political system. These are elected leaders, or in some cases, self-selected leaders.

The dotted boxes represent the environment within which these people act, and I divide the environment into domestic environment and external environment or international arena. I hypothesize – and I think it is the working assumption of organizations with population assistance – that influence in the form of supports or demands from the international environment can force nations to act in a certain way.

Specifically, my research deals with Latin America. I've taken the traditional countries of Latin America, excluding the British and French Caribbean, because they're special cases and not really Latin America. There are three specific questions which I want to speak to very briefly this afternoon.

The first is: which are the organizations seeking to influence population policy in Latin America? A question which on its face may seem easy to answer, but in fact is very confusing.

Secondly, what are they doing? How are they seeking to influence policy?

And thirdly, is there any indication that they've had any effect? (See Table 4).

Now, going to the first question, in Table 1, I've simply tried to enumerate the organizations involved in Latin America, and to classify them according to their legal status and some other characteristics. I'll try to explain my organizational categories.

There are bilateral public programs, multilateral public programs, and private programs of various types. These categories are based upon legal differences with important political implications. As we all know, there is an on-going debate regarding the effectiveness of multilateral foreign assistance as opposed to bilateral foreign assistance. This debate carries over into the various advantages and disadvantages of public assistance versus private assistance, particularly in the population field, because it is argued that an issue as controversial as population should be dealt with in as low a profile as possible; therefore, a heavier reliance upon private organizations, and multilateral organizations. That's the rationale of people who take this position.

The only kind of organization I haven't considered, which may be of significance in the future, is the commercial operation.

All right, let me make a few generalizations about the first question, that is, about the identity of the organizations.

The first thing we can say – and that's obvious from what the preceding speakers have said – is that there's been a tremendous expansion in the amount and variety of assistance available for population control and family planning. I have a figure which says that in 1962 the total amount of foreign aid available, obligated foreign aid, was in the neighborhood of $5 million. In 1969, and this is obligated money – money which is actually appropriated – the amount was $95 million, an increase of almost twenty-fold, and it's going higher.

Not so many years ago, in the early 1960's, the only sources of external assistance for family planning were private, and came from the Scandinavian countries – particularly Sweden. In the mid-1960's, the United States became involved, and, as is the case with many of these things when we get involved in something, we become more Catholic than the Pope, if I may indulge in that metaphor. Once committed, the United States began encouraging developed countries and international agencies to become more involved. So the multilateral agencies committed funds for population assistance and private organizations tremendously increased their activities.

A second observation in this realm would be that the source of this change at the international level was the result of a work by a fairly small number of people, people in the United States Congress, for example: Senator Gruening of Alaska, who was very important. There were a number of citizens who were also active. This indicates to me that even on the international level, relatively few well-placed individuals can have a lot of influence.

And a third observation, or tentative finding, would be that this rapid expansion has not occurred without problems. There has been internal stress within the organizations; these are organizations in some cases which had small budgets and small staffs, and within two or three years their budgets and staffs are tripled and sometimes increased by tenfold.

There is also a problem of overlap, and lack of coordination among these organizations at the international and regional levels.

The final observation, which is somewhat superfluous because of what Mr. Claxton has said, is that the United States has played the most important – the key – the overwhelming role in this whole expansion of international population assistance. According to the figures I have, which come from an OECD study, in 1969, roughly one-half of the total amount of foreign assistance available for population was supplied by the United States. I think that figure is somewhat understated, for a number of reasons. And this expansion of U.S. activity comes at a time when our overall foreign aid budget is declining, so that within the foreign aid programs of the United States, population-oriented assistance is assuming – although it's only 5% – a fairly significant role.

Well, let me talk a little bit about what these organizations do with their money, which is their primary resource. In Table 1, I've tried to develop functional categories that have some theoretical significance; that is, it seems to me that the kinds of activities and functions that I've indicated along the top are functions which are in some sense logically necessary for a country to act upon its population problem.

And secondly, the functional categories are empirically justified because these are the kinds of activities the international organizations engage in.

As to findings regarding types of functions, very few international organizations of any kind engage in direct local action, and by "direct local action" I mean the delivery of goods and services to local consumers, operating family planning clinics, for example. It's just too controversial to be done by any kind of foreign agency.

The second category, that of research, is concerned with providing the knowledge base for action. We have to know certain things before we can act. We've talkedabout this in a technological sense. Medical research generates basic knowledge about human reproduction essential to population control, but non-medical social science research in fields like demography, social attitudes, and economic development has recently become very important also. Most of the expansion into the latter has been financed by the agencies listed on Table 1.

There's also been a shift from pure research to applied research, for example, research which uses previous pure research having to do with female reproduction, or even more esoteric topics, to design a better contraceptive or to, more importantly, design better delivery systems.

It seems to me that local research, research which these organizations do in a given underdeveloped country, is often done for two reasons: first of all, to advance knowledge about population matters, and secondly it is a means of "keeping the foot in the door." It's a means of sensitizing the specialists of an underdeveloped area to population problems. In some cases I think this is much more important than the first objective.

Related to research is the third function of education and training, and here we're concerned about the human resource phase, the skilled manpower base to run a family planning program or implement a national population policy. The emphasis is on training, mainly because of the way I've categorized it, most education in a professional sense is done at the university level. The foundations and AID are particularly important in supporting people for advanced degrees, but they also have training programs – short-term programs – which give professional medical people, para-medical people, certain skills to deal with population.

I would argue that education and training is another kind of activity that international organizations use to sensitize nationals from the less-developed countries to their population problems. And also, I think technical assistance, which is my fourth categorical function, serves the same purpose.

Two functions remain – two final functions, or services, which international organizations provide. The first one is information and promotion. And what I'm talking about here is a form of lobbying, I guess, local lobbying by international organizations. And this is one of the two key activities of international organizations, that of disseminating information with the idea of promoting action on the population issue. Targets of this lobbying activity can be the general public, opinion leaders, government officials, political figures and specialists of various kinds. The means used by these organizations are mass communications, special publications, seminars, very much like this one, symposiums, conferences and all kinds of informal contacts that take place between officials in these organizations and officials at the national level.

There are several organizations which are devoted exclusively to this lobbying activity at international levels: in Latin America, one of the most important is the Population Reference Bureau, which has its home office in Washington, D.C.

One of the problems in regard to information and promotion is the kind of information explosion which we today have on population; there's so much information coming in it is almost impossible to handle. And some of the organizations are currently gearing up to coordinate the dissemination of information.

The final category is that of financial and material assistance, which simply means funding all the other activities that we've talked about. Organizations like AID, Ford, and Rockefeller are not operating agencies; they finance activities by other agencies.

The single most important source of international funding is AID; then come the American foundations, and the UN Trust Fund. In the Western Hemisphere, the World Bank and the Inter-American Development Bank provide some financial assistance.

Let me try to indicate the impact of all this activity very briefly. The final chart I have is Table 2, which correlates the organizations with the countries in which they are active. Let me just give some tentative findings which can be illustrated by this chart. (See Table 3).

In the first place, virtually all countries in Latin America receive some outside assistance, even Cuba. In the second place, the most active organizations are, first of all, AID, in terms of U.S. presence in countries and money spent, and secondly, private organizations.

The significance of this is, I think, that the multilateral organizations, be they international or regional, have been reluctant to move into Latin America, where population is still fairly controversial. They are, however, increasing their support under pressure from the United States.

Now, the private organizations are particularly important in Latin America, because they can act and provide assistance in certain countries where public agencies are not permitted to act. These are countries like Brazil, Argentina, Peru, and Mexico; Brazil and Mexico are the two important cases, large countries with high birth-rates, which have nominally pro-natalist population policies.

The international anti-natalist lobby, if we can use that term, keeps its foot in the door in this case through the private foundations and organizations like Population Council and IPPF. And in some cases, AID money goes to these countries through these private intermediaries.

In those countries which have adopted population policies, and which are officially anti-natalist, or at least support active family planning programs, there seems to be a very high correlation between external assistance and the policy itself. And these are countries like Chile, Costa Rica and Colombia, which have very active programs and draw a great deal of external assistance.

There's also evidence from countries that are just beginning to move in the direction of birth control and population planning, that the promise of financial assistance – we might call these financial inducements – and certain implicit demands made by the international agencies can lead to a shift in national population policies. This is the case in the Dominican Republic, Ecuador and El Salvador.

For those of you who are interested, I have some budget data on El Salvador, which indicates that the role of international agencies is overwhelming in the family planning program. And it was overwhelming at a very crucial time.

So one could, I think, conclude that the international agencies and international population organizations' programs have had a really significant impact. It is an impact which is reversible, however. We have a few examples of countries that have adopted anit-natalist postures, and then reversed themselves.

The best example that I know of in Latin America is Peru, which was moving in that anti-natalist direction in 1968; it had a fairly heavy commitment from Ford Foundation and from other sources. But with an unscheduled change in governments, as occurs frequently in Latin America – in this case a military coup – the new government backed off completely and the trend was reversed.

I would argue that one of the factors which can force a reversal in population policy, if you will, which can serve as a negative input from the international environment is too much pressure from outside. Particularly from the United States, in the case of the Western Hemisphere, and I think this is a consideration that has to be made when we discuss international support for population control.

UNITED NATIONS POPULATION ACTIVITIES

*By John Keppel**

As a representative of a development assistance donor agency in the population field, which is what the UNFPA is, I might begin by making an observation about the rationale or the possible effect of external assistance in the population field in general. That is that decision-makers and political figures in the less-developed countries are often well aware of the many effects of a rapid rate of population growth, and in some cases, of the effects of very high rates of population density on various forms of welfare and progress. In many cases, these effects are relatively long-term. Yet this is not always so; a new-born child demands medical care, it demands nutrition, it puts some pressures on the political and economic system, but that pressure is not nearly as great as that exerted by a young adult some years later, who demands employment, is vocal, and is a force to be reckoned with, as a potential voter and a potential rioter. So this delayed effect of population growth, or partially delayed effect, often serves in the cosmos of a populated world to call attention to the fact that some controls are desirable.

On the local level, a leader is swayed in the dilemma by pressures regarding the use of local resources. Many of these resource-oriented stresses are very short-term in their influence on his future as an individual decision-maker. Even though he knows that population growth is important in the long run, he often finds it difficult to devote scarce resources to population programs, even

*United Nations Fund for Population Activities.

though the long-range considerations urge him to do so. This fact of life is one of the underlying reasons for development assistance in population-related fields.

Of course, the aim of development policies and programs is to apply the external resources locally but not obviate the need for complementary internal resource application. Therefore, external aid is used as an inducement for the local government to apply its resources with the hope of getting more from the outside for their own willingness to put up some of their own.

Now, let's consider the efforts of the UN system in the area of population action. While the UN system has been having a certain amount of influence in the world, in the demographic field, and in terms of projections of population growth, having an influence perhaps on people's conceptions about the population problem, and having some influence through multilateral bodies on population policies, in terms of a development assistance system, it is only a recent participant. As a newcomer, we use other people's resources, which they donate to us; we often use their conceptual schemes, we use their technology, in many cases we use their training systems, by borrowing or sometimes hiring their personnel. Indeed, with regard to the UN system, there is some justification for doing this. Especially since the potential utility of the system for dealing with the population problem is relatively obvious to most nations. Thus it is one in which most nations feel some sense of participation; they do not look upon it with peculiar suspicion, as the Fund has no ulterior motivation.

With the Population Fund a new start is being made in specifically developing assistance in the population field; a new start which will hopefully lead to world-wide involvement.

However, the system has characteristics which must be taken into account while attempting to visualize what it has done and what it can do in the population field. It is worth focusing on the fact that there are a number of organizations in the UN system that are quite relevant here – the United Nations Secretariat itself, and its Economic Commissions, which come under its own general mandate. These organizations have a considerably broad mandate for the acquisition of demographic statistics, demographic projections, for the formulation of demographic predictions and data for economic and social planning, for the development of population policies, and for the evaluation of population programs. WHO, the World Health Organization, of course, has a mandate, or a degree of expertise in any event, in the field of the health aspects of population growth and distribution. UNESCO, the educational, scientific and cultural organization, has competency in various aspects of communication, education, and science. ILO, the labor organization, and FAO, the agricultural organization, have specialized clientele, sometimes of great importance – the farmers in one case and the labor organizations and employees in the other – which are crucially important audiences. UNICEF, with a concern for mother and child welfare, has become active in the population field. And finally the World Bank is engaged in developmental problems which require analysis of the population trends of the member nations.

Now all of these organizations have their own governing bodies, they have their own mandates, and they have their own regular budgets. Yet, we are all covered with the one blue flag, and it becomes a complex system of relatively sovereign international organizations.

In looking at what the system has done, I distinguish two streams of action, which are relevant to what I just said. One is the kind of action which has developed directly from the resolutions of intergovermental bodies, the governing bodies of these various organizations. And the other stream of action is one less clearly related to it; these are usually mutually supportive streams of action.

Ever since 1947, when the Population Commission was instituted, the United Nations Secretariat has been active in the field of demographic statistics and their related implications.

However, since there are many members of the international community, a substantial number on a decreasing scale, who had reservations about family planning, fertility reduction, as a form of governmental policy or a form of United Nations policy, it was harder to get into the family planning/fertility reduction field than into the demographic field. We have already seen how a limited amount of opposition can prevent a fully intergovernmental body from taking an action which would have been based on a consensus rather than a vote.

This illustrates one of the characteristics of this fully legislative, fully intergovernmental, stream of action. Yet we ought not scoff at these setbacks as many nations are participating in the process, and, thus, the channel of communications to them from whatever actions the UN system takes functions more easily through to their own member governments.

Despite these characteristics, as more attention came to the population problems of the world, the specialized agencies – WHO, ILO – in the system began to acquire mandates; that is, legislative actions by their own governing bodies, which permitted them to promulgate action programs in the family planning field, as well as other aspects of population. However, this didn't immediately lead them to adopt effective large-scale delivery systems for family planning assistance programs. This occurred for several reasons; one being that while the governing bodies did come to agreements about the mandates, they were merely mandates which couldn't be executed without funds. The Secretaries of these bodies, rightly or wrongly, didn't feel that they could get those funds out of the governing bodies, even though they had the mandate.

Moreover, there was a second impeding factor which I'm sure was just as important: like any bureaucratic organization, all of the UN organizations had existing personnel, existing structures, existing tables of organization, and they had vested interests in the on-going programs. The technique used inside the United States to alter this ranking of priorities inside the existing bureaucratic structures was the specific earmarking of part of the foreign assistance budget for use in the area of population control. Perhaps with that model in mind, the Secretary General, in 1967, despite this progress in the UN system in getting broader mandates, decided that more ought to be done, and he established the UN Fund for Population Activities, as a single source of extra-budgetary, non-competitive funds within the system. Later, he vested control of this fund in the United Nations Development Program, hoping thereby to take advantage of the existent field apparatus, the managerial skills, and the established potential for inter-organizational coordination.

This year the Fund will have an operating budget of about $25 million. We have some twenty-four donors, twenty-three in addition to the United States. The Fund is not an executing organization; its programs are executed primarily by the organizations in the UN system with the substantive mandate in the various fields, programs of education, health, development are utilized as modes of achieving the goals of the Fund. However, it is free to use organizations outside the UN system; if so desired, it is free to work with the International Planned Parenthood Federation, or with women's organizations or with any other non-governmental organizations.

In conclusion, we are engaged in a large-scale trial of the capacity of the system to develop, to deliver a useful assistance promptly and efficiently to those developing countries which need, want and request it. To the extent that donor nations and recipient nations more fully utilize the capabilities of the Fund's population assistance program, the governmental mandates and the local aspirations for well-being will be realized.

THE CASE FOR COMPULSORY REGULATION OF REPRODUCTION

*By Johnson C. Montgomery**

One would have thought, with all of the experts here today, that we could present some sort of picture of success, but unfortunately there is no point at which these population policies have succeeded. There's no place in the world that presently has a zero population growth.

This is an intelligent audience; the audience knows what the facts are. Yet sometimes we're prone to forget them. We're likely to forget how short the doubling time has become – how fast this bomb is ticking and how catastrophically it is apt to go off. I think that even those people who deal with the problems of population growth every day forget the imminent threat. I won't review the statistics, because I assume that with a simple reminder, you'll remember what a foreboding picture they present. What is important is to look at the basic causes , because if we understand the causes, we'll more fully understand how difficult it is to make a real difference. One cause of the population crisis is that during most of the history of man's evolution, his principal problem, scrabbling on the face of the earth, has been to increase population size. Genetic and cultural evolution favored this. The consequence of this is that now we are faced with the results of man's reproductive success.

***Counsel for Zero Population Growth**

We have over the years built into our social systems a great deal of inertia. There are a lot of mechanisms that are specifically designed to make change occur slowly, especially in our institutions. For example, our own Constitution is not easily amended. Moreover, it is difficult to get people to change their minds when all of our social institutions have developed on the basis that it was highly desirable to reproduce profusely.

Differential Reproduction Rates

There are a number of additional problems which have not yet been mentioned. One of them, which touches upon what kinds of policies we can implement, deserves special attention – the problem of differential reproduction. Different groups, different individuals, have more children than others. There are different groups that are growing at faster rates than others. There are different nations growing at faster rates than others. Such circumstances create a potentially explosive political and social atmosphere. According to the United Nations preliminary projections for population growth between now and the year 2000, the United States population is going to grow by about 70 per cent; Latin America, which is already grossly overpopulated, is going to grow by 170 percent; Europe is going to grow by about 32 percent; Africa by 150 percent; the Soviet Union by less than 100 percent; and the Indian and Asian countries by over 200 percent. The growth of population in China and the Arab nations directly threatens their neighbors, and it increases international tensions. It certainly tends to increase the risk of thermonuclear disaster.

Within individual nations, differential reproduction rates also cause a real problem. Not many people realize it, but in 1790, when the first census was taken, the United States had almost 20 percent Negroes. That percentage declined to a low of 9.7 percent in 1930, according to our census figures, and is now on the way up again. This year, white children in the Los Angeles City Schools became a minority for the first time. And this was cause for a lot of comment, a lot of concern. There was a very alarming editorial in the Los Angeles Times about that. Probably nobody wants to be forced to be part of a minority.

Another, more striking example is what has happened in South Africa. In 1795, they had about one-third white; about one-third natives – that would be the Bantus, who, of course, immigrated into South Africa much earlier than the whites; and one-third actual natives – the Hottentots and bushmen. By 1960, the figures were three million whites, 11 million natives, plus one and a half million colored. And during that decade of the 50's, the whites increased their population in South Africa by 16 percent, while the blacks increased theirs by 26 percent. In South Africa, the present birth rate for whites is 22 percent, approximately; for coloreds, the birth rate is 46 percent.

If we start extrapolating, in 150 years the blacks would be a majority in the United States. That scares people. Now when we analyze what we are going to do about the population problem, we must take into consideration this fact of differential reproduction.

We know differential reproduction has to some extent contributed to the erosion of civil liberties in South Africa, and I hate to think what will happen in this country if we don't come to some reasonable way of solving the problem.

Unrealistic Solutions

Now almost everyone here has talked about family planning, as if that's the way this problem is going to be solved. I'd classify family planning much the same way I classify other unrealistic solutions, such as sending our population off in space ships to other planets. We know that the popular expectations of looking to the oceans, to the deserts, to the lateritic soils in the equatorial areas, aren't going to solve our basic problem. Pasting bandaids on what is essentially a man who's bleeding to death will not solve the problem. That's what family planning is in my opinion.

The basic problem comes to one fact: we've got to get population growth to zero. In fact, in long-range terms, we should probably reduce the size of the world's human population. Two and a half children per reproductive woman is not low enough. It's got to go down to zero, maybe lower. And the fact of the matter is simply that right now people want to have too many children. The reason we all want to have too many children is because we were selected for this over thousands and thousands of years.

A study at Cornell, where we were dealing presumably with highly educated and responsible people, showed that 65 percent wanted three or more children. We can't continue to have three or more children per family; we just all can't do it, and yet that is what most of us want. Even if each living woman in the United States today gives birth to only one female child, who survives to reproductive age, we're still going to reach 300 million by the year 2045.

Now, that may sound like a long way off, but when you look at that population growth curve and realize what happened during the period from about 1650 to the present, you'll realize we are facing an absolute disaster, and we cannot rely solely on good intentions, or on feelings of responsibility. Responsibility hasn't worked in the past and I don't think it's going to work in the future.

A recent Gallup Poll shows that 23 percent of the American public thinks four or more children is the ideal family size. In terms of what's going on in the United States today, are we going to plan families so that these 23 percent have four or more children? If we do, there's not going to be any world left for any of us, or any of our children.

The Role of Law in Solving the Problem

The role of law has not been very carefully analyzed, but I want to make a few comments on what I perceive to be the particularly important fundamental legal questions that have to do with the right to have children, the rights of the fetus, and the equal protection issues.

We should observe at the threshold in this inquiry that whatever our rules of law, nature does issue the last edicts, and she may disregard anything that human beings decide. If our policies aren't sensible, she is going to issue a last edict, and it could be an edict which exterminates us.

The Right to Found a Family

Now, what about the right to have children? The right to found a family? There has been a good deal said about that, and I think the most important language in the international agreements has already been quoted to you, but there are a couple of things I'd like to emphasize.

First, the Universal Declaration of Human Rights provides that:

> Men and women of full age, without limitation due to race, nationality or religion, have the right to marry and found a family.

You can read that as meaning that you cannot have population control based upon discrimination – race, nationality, or religion. But some other basis for population control, even compulsory control, would be acceptable.

Second, the declaration by the world leaders which was quoted at length here, was also included as part of a resolution at the United Nations. Actually, it was part of the United Nations Declaration on Social Progress and Development. The declaration states that "parents have the exclusive right to determine freely and responsibly the number and spacing of their children."

That's not an unlimited license that permits three children. Your right extends only to responsible reproduction. This entire planet is a single eco-system; we all rely upon it for our life support systems; and until we are all exercising reproduction in a responsible way, it's neither just nor fair to ask any one of us to do so.

There may be a right to have one child; that's part of the right to have children. There may be a right to reproduce yourself, which would permit two offspring for a couple. There may be a right to have both a boy and a girl, and this was mentioned as a possible problem earlier. Incidentally, technology is doing something about that; there are now methods which will enable us to have some control over sex determination.

There may have once been a right to have as many children as you want; in fact, there was once a responsibility that each human being have as many kids as he could possibly have, to keep the human race going. But that right, that duty, no longer exists. We face an entirely different factual situation today than we were facing earlier in history; we've got to understand this, and we've got to change our basic institutions. We must think about reproduction not as a right but as a privilege. That privilege must be exercised responsibly.

Rights of the Fetus

Now, what about the fetus? In the United States, and in other countries, we often hear the argument that "the fetus has a right to life." I've investigated this as carefully as I can under Anglo-American law, and I don't find any right to life that a fetus has.

The dual argument is often made that human life begins at conception and that we value human life. There is no question about the last part of it: we do value human life. Our task is to give dignity, meaning and decency to each human being who is alive. But that doesn't mean we have to overload this planet so that none of us has a decent life; and the fetus, when we look at it properly, is not a beginning of human life. Life does not begin at conception.

If there's one thing scientists, theologians, and moralists agree upon, it is that human life doesn't begin at all. It began. It began at some moment far in the past; whether by an act of Divine Creation, or a coming up through the colloidal slime, it began in the past. The egg is nothing but a continuation of an adult. And the fertilized egg is nothing but a continuation of the sperm and egg, and the fetus is nothing but a continuation of the fertilized egg. And the infant a continuation of the fetus, the child a continuation of the infant, and so forth, to adulthood.

Notice one thing: every society in history has accorded different rights, different protections to different stages of human life. A child is not given the same rights as an adult, nor does he have the same duties. And so the mere fact that a fetus happens to be living doesn't mean that the fetus has a "right to life" any more than my individual cells have a right to life – or my germinal cells for that matter.

The real question is: at what stage do we want to protect human life, and for what purposes? We haven't protected fetuses in the past. At this late date in history, I do not believe we should extend a right of life to a fetus.

The most logical time at which to extend protection is birth; that is the time from which we date all other legal consequences – social security rights, driver's licenses, draft obligations, and so forth. Essentially, all human time span is measured from birth, and I think that is the appropriate time at which to attach rights.

Government Power to Control Population

I submit there is ample governmental power to control population. In the United States, we can regulate population under the Commerce Clause, under the Welfare Clause, and probably under Section 5 of the 14th Amendment. The question is: how do we want to do it? The basic issue is that of equal protection.

The Use of Compulsion

I submit that we cannot permit anyone to reproduce irresponsibly, and by that I mean have more than his fair share of children, who will be limited to their fair share of the world's resources. If we permit any one person to do it, we can't ask anyone else to exercise responsibility. This inevitably means that we are going to face a form of compulsion. Compulsion is a dirty word; it deserves some scrutiny.

When I try to persuade someone to do something, that is a form of compulsion. Some people are compelled by watching the nonsense on TV to go out and buy things they don't want, didn't need, and didn't even know about. That is a form of compulsion. In a sense, that is as compelling as telling a man he can only have one wife, or a woman that she can have only one husband. Since we can tell people how many spouses they can have, and since most nations do just that, I think we have some legal authority for telling people how many children they can have.

There is a very interesting book which explores this type of fertility control. It was written by Ed Chasteen, called *The Case for Compulsory Birth Control.*

Chasteen recommends a law which would be applicable only in the United States – but with potential worldwide application. The law would say that no person shall have more than two children – no woman shall have more than two children. He further hypothesizes the development of technology to give a woman who has exceeded her limit a vaccination thus immunizing her against future pregnancies.

We don't have that kind of technology today, but assuming

that we did have it, how about that proposal? It is basically a fair proposal. My own proposal, ten years ago, was to control reproduction with non-assignable licenses. A license to reproduce that can be sold would be useless because then the rich would be rewarded at the expense of the poor. So non-assignable licenses are the answer. If it were necessary – if we were faced with an immediate catastrophe tomorrow – we would have no problem justifying compulsory birth control, perhaps reinforced by compulsory abortion. I think the law will permit that when there is a clear and present danger of crisis.

It is my opinion that the crisis is clear enough right now to justify certain forms of what everyone thinks of as compulsion. We should limit people to two children, perhaps even to fewer, because right now, as a result of the age composition of the world's population, we cannot stabilize our population at the present level simply by having everyone have two children. There are too many young people who are entering the reproduction age, so that the ultimate world population, even if only two children were born to each woman, would still be far in excess of what it is today. We may have to set the limit at one child per couple.

I might point out, since there are attorneys here, that the cases which hold that the principle of choice is a basic human right say without exception that absent a compelling, subordinating interest, we have a right to choose how many children we want. But I submit that there is a compelling, subordinating interest right now. However, the courts may not recognize this at present. Inertia has been built into their systems too. It will take time, and it may take a real tragedy, but the discussions that we've heard today about how hard it is to change people's minds are going to become irrelevant when we meet catastrophe.

Toward a Real Solution to the Problem

In conclusion, it is popular today to characterize certain suggested methods of population control as voluntary and others as compulsory. Thus education, economic incentives and removal of restrictions on contraception, sterilization and abortion have been characterized as voluntary, whereas licensing births and criminal laws requiring contraception, sterilization and abortion have been characterized as compulsory. It may be that the distinction between voluntary and compulsory methods does not advance the analysis and will not assist in developing effective, fair programs for controlling population size. Suppose a person wants ten children but is persuaded by media and public attitudes that ten is too many. It can be argued that the person has been subjected to a form of compulsion. Similarly it can be argues that licensing births is no more "compulsory" than licensing marriages.

The basic question appears to be: what programs will be both effective and non-discriminatory? The next question is: which programs appear to have public acceptance? It is submitted that the most effective, non-discriminatory program would involve direct governmental regulation of reproduction. A statute could be passed prohibiting any person from having more than two children and the penalty for unauthorized conception would be compulsory abortion. In the long run, direct regulation of reproduction may be the only way to ensure effective control of population size. It is probably the only device by which the problems of differential reproduction can be solved. However, direct regulation of reproduction is not presently popular and probably will not become popular until a population-related catastrophe occurs. Meanwhile, to mitigate the misery which will be caused by the catastrophe, we must immediately enact those population control measures which do have substantial public support. These measures include a world-wide educational campaign; a world-wide family planning program; extensive research and development programs to facilitate contraception, abortion and sterilization; the enactment of economic incentives and disincentives; and the repeal of all laws limiting contraception, abortion and sterilization. These measures may not be fair, and, they probably won't work in the long run; but we should apply them immediately. We may hope for the best, but we must plan for the worst.

LEGAL IMPEDIMENTS TO VOLUNTARISM

*By Harriet F. Pilpel**

I have a totally different frame of reference, not only from the directly preceding speakers but to a considerable extent from any of the speeches we've heard. It all has to do with what we understand to be the basic problem: voluntary control of fertility.

I disagree that voluntarism can be compared with putting bandaids on a jugular vein, and I think that if most of what Mr. Montgomery had to say were translated into the area of food and hunger, it would be like saying that the solution for hunger is to prohibit people from starving! That might sound like a very good thing to do, but it is doubtful that it would work. I think the solution to the population problem is not to prohibit people from having more than one or two children, but to make it possible for them to have as many children as they need and want in the light, not only of their personal desires, but in the light of the needs of the society in which they live.

What I really want, I guess, Dr. Ravenholt, is an AID program for the United States. We need, at least as much as any other country in the world needs, a program here to make voluntarism possible, because, contrary to popular belief, we have never really had voluntarism in family planning in the U.S.

Many years ago, when those of us who are so old we can remember, we went into the courts to fight for the availability of birth control without any awareness of a population problem. We didn't know we were the advance troops for population limitation. We thought we were fighting for the constitutional freedoms of the individual and for public health, and we found that we were facing a series of laws and institutions that made it virtually impossible for the poor and quite difficult for the well-to-do to have only the children they wanted.

Oddly enough, that situation, after thirty-odd years of battling on the part of Planned Parenthood, the Civil Liberties Union and many others, has not been very substantially changed. I would

*Senior partner, Greenbaum, Wolff and Ernst; Counsel to Planned Parenthood-World Population.

suggest to Mr. Montgomery that what we need here is a program to make voluntarism possible in the United States. If we succeeded in that, then I think Dr. Ravenholt would be right not only in preaching freedom of choice, but in saying that in the United States we are "exemplars" of freedom of choice. With all due deference, I'm not at all sure, in view of our present legal structure, that we are yet that.

Now, since I am the last speaker, and have very limited time, I will make five points briefly.

I should first identify the pro-natalist laws we have on our books, the laws which interfere with freedom of choice in family planning. Then I would like to briefly talk about the necessity to publicize those laws so people will know they exist – I sometimes wonder if Mr. Montgomery and many of the ZPG people really know that these laws are on the books. In the third place, I'd like to show, again disagreeing with Mr. Montgomery, that these laws are not reflective of what the population of the United States wants by any means, but rather – taking the words of Phyllis Piotrow – that the American people don't want them, but haven't had the knowledge or power to change them.

I'd like to show also that where these laws have been changed, either in the United States or elsewhere, population growth rates have been substantially reduced. Finally, I'd like to urge (which I can do since I'm not myself a tax-exempt institution) that we get rid of these pro-natalist laws and give voluntarism a chance to work.

Now, just to mention a few of the pro-natalist laws on our books. We may pride ourselves that after ninety-eight years, we, last month, repealed the Federal Comstock Laws, which prohibited the importation, transportation and mailing of, and I quote: "any article whatever for the prevention of conception." Despite many efforts to get the Comstock laws off the books, they just stayed there.

It is true that via Planned Parenthood and other agencies, a number of lawyers, including several from my own office, were able to get them interpreted almost out of existence. But they still were a trap for the unwary, as various manufacturers and clinics discovered when they tried to send contraceptives through the mails. Cases have arisen in the last decade, where Post Office Department personnel have prohibited clinics, doctors, and manufacturers from sending contraceptives through the mails to people who asked for them. Such problems still arise to plague us because although the Comstock Laws have been repealed, Congress has left, in effect, a "dangling participle," which prohibits the mailing or shipment in interstate commerce of unsolicited advertisements of contraceptives, and unsolicited contraceptives. Yes, as I said, we got rid of a few hundred-year-old laws, but tacked onto their repeal this crippling limitation, which we may have to live with for another hundred years if we live that long.

Those of you who work in family planning programs know that one of the only ways of reaching otherwise unreachable target groups in the United States who want birth control help and don't have it is by unsolicited mailings of advertisements of contraceptives and of contraceptives themselves. This is true, for example, with reference to migrant workers, some student populations and others.

Another example: in New York, we have a law that sounds liberal and provides that anybody sixteen and over can purchase contraceptives in a drugstore. But the display of contraceptives even in drugstores is prohibited in New York, as is the advertisement of contraceptives; again a very serious impediment to any kind of an intensive population education or family planning campaign.

Massachusetts and Wisconsin still prohibit the distribution of contraceptives to the unmarried. The validity of the Massachusetts law is involved in a case now pending before the United States Supreme Court, so all we can do in this day and age is hope and work for a decision that such laws are clearly unconstitutional. Mississippi and Louisiana, in a sense, have adopted Mr. Montgomery's suggestions. They make it criminal to have more than one illegitimate child. But at the same time, Mississippi makes it illegal to sell contraceptives. They obviously are in favor of abstinence, or some other highly moralistic approach.

Notwithstanding the Louisiana law, a project in Louisiana has demonstrated – as I'll point out in a moment – that where you make family planning possible to a given population that didn't have access to it, you can greatly reduce the rate of population growth.

Finally, and I'm sorry I haven't time to identify all the pro-natalist laws , I want to mention that the laws as to distribution of contraceptives to minors and medical treatment of minors in this country hark back to the 19th century. It is only now in the 1970's that we are beginning to make it possible for minors, usually defined as anyone under twenty-one, to get absolutely necessary medical treatment even without parental consent in the areas of venereal disease, in particular, and family planning, in general.

So much for examples of some of the pro-natalist laws we stubbornly maintain on our books.

Next question: have we publicized those laws? We certainly have not. We've had a massive campaign on cigarette smoking, which I guess has done something. Every Post Office has big signs saying: "If you don't want pornographic material, just send this in...", part of a very elaborate promotional structure to keep our minds free from obscenity.

I would suggest that if we used either the Madison Avenue techniques of cigarette advertising – pro or con – or the kind of governmental campaign the Post Office launched against obscenity to make family planning services and information available, there'd be no need for talk about compulsory population control. However, laws are being proposed which unfortunately reflect the kind of views expressed by Mr. Montgomery – for example, the bill introduced in the legislature of the State of Hawaii makes sterilization compulsory for any woman who has two living children. (Fortunately, there doesn't seem to be any chance of its passing.)

We're struggling in New York now with an opinion of the Attorney General that says Medicaid is not available for voluntary elective sterilization. Since voluntary sterilization is an important and effective method of birth control (about two million people have had sterilization operations in the U.S.–several hundred thousand vasectomies were done last year) it does seem odd that Medicaid should be withheld for such an operation in a state like New York, and we expect to challenge that ruling in a test case.

In addition to maintaining pro-natalist laws, and tolerating a total lack of publicity and public education with reference to them, we do little to make known the fact that most people don't want them and are hurt by them. Some of the statistics have already been cited: 22 percent of the children born in this country are, according to the Westoff studies, unwanted. The recent Gallup Poll, referred to by Mr. Montgomery, shows not so much that 23 percent of the people polled wanted four or more children but that 77 percent wanted fewer than four and that seems to me a more significant statistic.

In general, it seems clear to me that if there were a popular referendum on any of these laws, such as there was in the state of Washington on abortion, you would have a majority in favor of freedom of choice, of getting these pro-natalist laws off the books. The people in Washington did not think they would win their abortion referendum, and in fact were very apprehensive about it, but they did win it by a vote of 56 percent. At the risk of being very rash, I will say that I am certain that a referendum on any of these laws would call for their repeal everywhere in the United States. If only we did have the means to get this submitted to the people instead of having it languish in our legislative halls, progress would be more rapid.

Fourth, I want to point out that where the laws and practices against freedom of choice in family planning have been changed, the birth rate has been reduced. When Japan made abortion available, its population growth rate was halved in a decade. In New York, from July 1st to December 31st, the ratio of live births to abortions in the state was one to one; 69,000 abortions were performed in New York City alone after the repeal law went into effect,many of themon out-of-towners (Thus the 1 to 1 ratio does not reflect the situation as to New York residents.)*

New York is the only state which has repealed its abortion law, and does not impose a rather severe residence requirement. Furthermore, it's the only state in the continental United States where abortion is generally available, except for the State of Washington, which is harder to get to.

If we identify the laws, publicize them, show that we don't want them, and show that their repeal has a substantial downward impact on our population growth rate, we will most probably end up with exhortation to get rid of them.

I don't think I have the time now to go into the details of how this can be done, but I do suggest that perhaps a whole conference might be devoted to that question. It is to me incredible that at a time when some are talking about compelling and coercing people not to have children they are not mentioning the fact that many people in this country are being compelled and coerced to have children they don't want. To punish them for what they can't help is not only a denial of due process and equal protection, but it also seems to be rank idiocy! It is also a source of dismay

* It is estimated that fully 169,000 abortions were performed in New York during the first full year after the repeal.

to me that as soon as the shoe pinches – we begin to talk about the necessity for modifying Constitutional guarantees. Our Constitutional guarantees exist mainly to protect minorities; majorities don't usually need them.

The theory behind the first ten amendments to our Constitution, including the 9th and 10th Amendments, which reserve certain rights to the people, is that if we allow Constitutional guarantees free play, we will not need any compulsory program. If we exercise our First Amendment rights, and really get a population education program going, we will, I am sure, demonstrate with Justice Holmes that the thought will get itself accepted in the marketplace. And if we protect and encourage real freedom by removing restrictions on freedom of choice in family planning, I don't think we'll have to change or modify any Constitutional guarantees.

Please bear in mind also that any such proposals as Mr. Montgomery has made couldn't possibly work. You can hardly force or coerce the entire country, and if we proceeded as he suggests, we would be punishing people who are not guilty of anything; we would no doubt be coming down more heavily on the minorities and the poor than we would on the rich, no matter how egalitarian the language of his proposal was.

In the final analysis, by using coercion you wouldn't be making a dent in the problem. I was on a platform recently with Mr. Chasteen, who wrote the book Mr. Montgomery referred to; he made the suggestion that all women who had had two children be vaccinated so they couldn't have more. I was timorous enough to ask what particular vaccine he had in mind, to which his response was, that that was a matter of detail and irrelevant to the basic issue. Well, I don't think it is a matter of detail, but since I'm glad to say we don't have such a vaccine, we don't need to discuss it.

The first case that I ever worked on was in the family planning field, before most of you were born. It involved the importation of contraceptives from Japan by Dr. Hannah Stone, an importation challenged as illegal under the old Comstock Laws. When I researched the issue as to whether a general statute prohibiting importation of contraceptives applied to a doctor, I found only two precedents. One of them was an ordinance in the city of Bologna, Italy in the 16th century, which held that a prohibition against a professional leech letting blood in the streets did not apply when a leech let blood for therapeutic purposes (which I regarded as a direct precedent).

The other had to do with the importation by Trinity Church of an esteemed Anglican minister who was said to fall within the general prohibition on the importation of contract labor. The United States Supreme Court said that the statute did not apply to the minister. And the Court in the Hannah Stone case similarly held that despite its absolute language, the prohibition of the importation of contraceptives did not apply to a physician.

Since the Hannah Stone case, we have developed some additional and helpful precedents, although really remarkably few. We are now in the position of having one case on abortion pending before the United States Supreme Court, which has been argued,* and several others there that may be sidestepped by the Court on procedural and technical grounds recently enunciated by the Court in cases that have nothing to do with abortion.

We have a number of states that have reformed rather than repealed their abortion laws, but as I said before, only four states have repealed their laws, and only one of them doesn't have a residence requirement.

We have the situation with respect to voluntary sterilization where, although the laws don't stand in the way, the medical profession and the hospitals are always worrying about being guilty of mayhem. When I went to law school, I learned that mayhem meant deliberately inflicting injury on oneself or another in a manner to interfere with that person's service to the King. This does not seem to me as relevant a precedent today as the leech law in Bologna, but it does apparently seem relevant to the members of the faculties of our medical schools, who I gather mention it in such a way as to make most difficult any real freedom of choice on voluntary sterilization, especially by the

*Since this paper was given the United States Supreme Court has handed down its decision in this case. The Court held that the District of Columbia statute which prohibits abortion except when necessary to preserve life or health of the woman is not unconstitutionally "vague." However, the case means a step toward greater freedom of choice in this area because the majority of the Court approved a very broad definition of health (physical and mental) and held that in a prosecution of a doctor for performing an abortion the burden of proof is on the government to prove beyond a reasonable doubt that the abortion was not necessary to preserve the life or health (thus broadly defined) of the woman. U.S. v. Vuitch, 402 U.S. ——, 91 S. Ct. 1294 (1971).

poor (a result also reached by the New York Attorney General's ruling on Medicaid I referred to before).

I'm sorry I don't have time to go into the laws and practices which make voluntary sterilization difficult to come by, except for people with money (and even occasionally the women in that group); the laws which keep abortion illegal, more or less, in forty-six out of fifty states; and the laws which prohibit the advertising and display and unsolicited dissemination of contraceptives and contraceptive advertising.

I will conclude by saying that whatever else we do anywhere in the world, if we can really become in the United States an exemplar of what a society is like where freedom of choice is possible, then I'm sure we'd never have to go beyond the question of freedom of choice. I am hopeful that the other nations in the world would be reassured and would then follow suit.

Discussion

Mr. John Atta Mills, of Ghana, took issue with several of the assertions made by Mr. Montgomery. There's no doubt in my mind that Mr. Montgomery is very sincere in his views about the advantages to be derived from the zero population growth. But I hope that I have misunderstood his speech, because certain reasons he adduced for getting a zero population program, in my view, only add to the armor of those who oppose the zero population program. I'm fully convinced that there is no law which limits the percentage of any particular group in any society. Every group has a right to wish for more than its share of the composition of its land. Therefore, I think that the reasons for a zero population growth should not be based upon a percentage composition in any particular group, but rather, upon some of the advantages which were put forward by the earlier speakers. As I said in the beginning, I hope this is only a mistake, that it is only a misunderstanding of his speech, because otherwise, the zero population program is going to run into a lot of difficulty.

Mr. Montgomery replied that he agreed with what was said, and in fact agreed with Mrs. Pilpel. He observed that the thing to keep in mind is this: that when we are looking at the legal framework in this country and elsewhere, we know that the government has power – if it doesn't have it, it will find it in order to do what is necessary; and if voluntary methods of population control do not work, and if leaving groups who want to increase their percentage share doesn't work, then we are either going to face the kind of catastrophe that has been described, or we are going to have to go on to compulsion. One of the reasons that I make the point of showing the legal case for compulsion is quite frankly to scare people into doing exactly what Mrs. Pilpel wants to be done. It's much easier to get somebody to compromise by repealing the abortion laws when they are threatened with impending doom. Now, tactically, this may be incorrect. To make things perfectly clear, ZPG is not and never has been on record as favoring compulsory population control. But there are real equal protection problems in all forms of population control. Yet, if we can solve it through voluntary methods, and no one feels that he is being discriminated against because someone else is going to outbreed him, then that's the solution we should have. There are still some areas in the world where they do not have a problem of overpopulation, where indeed they need more population – some of the areas in Africa, for example. Perhaps once the United States ceases to rip off their natural resources, they will have a chance for development.

Captain Jordan Paust of the Judge Advocate General's School. I still place my faith in international cooperative concern, but I would like to raise a point that hasn't been raised thus far. It pertains to the role of population control in international conflict management. Recognizing that some international conflicts, the Sino-Soviet border disputes, the Banana Revolution, and the Soccer Game War, may be classified as population wars, I would like to raise the issue, perhaps for further discussion later in the next panel, of the role of population control in conflict management, with the institutional framework for this inquiry being perhaps the General Assembly, or some other United Nations institution. I feel that we have neglected some of the relevance of this framework for international lawyer action.

Mr. Claxton felt that the statement obviously raised a most fundamental question, one which has barely begun to raise its head as a reality in international relations, but will become quite important as this century wears on and certainly into the next one. The Soccer War, as it has been called, between Honduras and El Salvador, is very clearly a population war, and was recognized as such in the Organization of American States when they considered action to try to restore peace in the area. The problem was that overpopulation and population pressure in El Salvador pushed many people into Honduras, where they took up living, began to occupy land, and became farmers, thus creating all the kinds of domestic irritation. A totally irrelevant episode in a soccer match between the two countries led to rioting which in turn broke out into warfare. But real irritation was primarily related to the situation of population movement from El Salvador into Honduras. There are a number of countries in Africa where precisely the same kind of thing is happening. As people from the poorer countries toward the interior have moved toward the countries on the West Coast, where there is a greater opportunity for making a living, some of the coastal states have begun, first to prohibit immigration, and secondly, and more recently, to push people back into the countries from which they came. The potential for serious trouble hardly needs to be emphasized. Happily, no real outburst has occurred yet, but as the populations continue to grow rapidly, in the interior countries and in the rural areas of Africa, the potential for real danger is obviously visible, especially where populations move into other countries. The only reason that this kind of issue has not arisen yet among large masses of different religions or different tribal extractions in many countries, or among nations, is that population growth control hasn't really succeeded in any of the countries that we're talking about yet.

But there are already degrees of irritation among the different religious groups in India, which are accentuated when one group in the majority tells all the groups that they should reduce their rate of population growth. The concern on the part of one group is: "Why are you telling us this? Are you trying to let the other group go ahead?" The same is true in some other countries; the same is true in some of the countries where tribal differences are important in individual countries. And the same will be true among different countries as population growth control begins to move more effectively, say, in one country, than in a neighbor country. This means that if minority groups are to safely, or in their own minds, to believe they're safe in reducing their rate of population growth, for the benefit of themselves and their children, there must be some assurance that they will be protected while remaining minorities; or if they are now a majority and they control their growth and some present minority becomes larger, there must be some assurance of some form of protection for their rights. This is going to be a major internal problem of a legal and constitutional nature in many countries, and in not too many decades, it will become a major international constitutional problem.

Whereupon the second panel was adjourned.

Third Session

Friday, March 12, 1971, at 8:00 p.m.

The World Population Crisis: Domestic and International Laws

The session convened at 8:00 p.m. in the East Hall of the School of Law, Professor Warren F. Schwartz, University of Virginia School of Law, presiding.

POPULATION-RELATED LAWS IN THE LESS-DEVELOPED COUNTRIES

*By Luke T. Lee**

Such a broadly drawn topic may appear as a rather impossible mission, especially when one considers the limitation of time placed upon us for such a discussion. In attempting the impossible, it will, therefore, be necessary to limit the range of the topic, at least geographically. I have accordingly chosen the continent of Africa as the case study; in view of the fact that I have just returned from an extended tour of that continent.

It will be useful at the outset to define the term "law" as it will be used by me this evening. When I speak of "law," I speak not only of constitutions, statutes, decrees, and judicial decisions, but also of governmental policies and programs. For the system in many of the developing countries is such that what the

*Director, Law and Population Programme, Fletcher School of Law and Diplomacy, Tufts University.

governments adopt as policy become their edicts. In effect, their programs are regarded as law.

From the viewpoint of population laws, the African countries can be divided into two categories: first, those which have felt the pressure of population growth and are therefore forced to change and develop laws which will aid them in the struggle of containing a burgeoning population – Tunisia, a Francophone country, and Ghana, an Anglophone state, are examples of this category; and second, those which have merely carried on or inherited laws or codes from the former colonial rulers, which are generally pro-natalist in nature – the Democratic Republic of the Congo is an example for the Francophone countries, and Nigeria is an example of the Anglophone states.

The extent of the changes introduced by Tunisia since independence may be seen as follows. It has raised the minimum marriage age, permitted abortion if the mother has five or more living children, legalized the sale of contraceptives, limited family allowances to the first four children of each family, and more importantly, outlawed polygamy – the first Moslem country to do so. The actual impact of these legal changes on the population is another matter to be discussed later perhaps.

Ghana, in 1969, adopted an official population policy called Population Planning for National Progress and Prosperity. Significant among the measures proposed is that set forth in Section 5-19, which should be relevant to our meeting tonight. It provided:

> Studies should be undertaken of the legal and the administrative structure and policies to ascertain ways in which they might be reoriented to reduce the pro-natalist influence and shift the weight of influence toward lower fertility. Import duties on contraceptive materials will be abolished .... Policies relating to maternity benefits, tax benefits for larger families, age at marriage, divorce and legal separation, and other areas relevant to fertility will be systematically examined and, if necessary, modified.

One important project, now in its final stages of planning, concerns the compulsory registration of vital statistics, which will be undertaken with UN assistance. It is a very ambitious and comprehensive project, which upon implementation will go a long way toward facilitating the Ghanean national family planning program.

I might add that during my visit to Ghana the ambitious intents of such a program proved to be genuine. Both government officials and university people expressed the sincere urgency of making these systematic evaluations and examinations with a view to adopting a comprehensive legal reform.

Upon turning to the countries which have inherited wholesale population laws of the former colonial countries, I should note that the difference between these countries and those just discussed is only a matter of degree.

For example, although Nigeria is still presently preoccupied with healing the wounds inflicted by the protracted civil war, it has already included in its Second National Development Plan 1970-74, a section on population policy which calls attention to the high population growth rate of 2.5 percent per year, the low per capita income, the high youth-dependency ratio, and the high rate of urbanization, as well as the high rates of urban and disguised unemployment.

As a result, the Government has pledged to "pursue a qualitative population policy by integrating the various voluntary family planning schemes into the overall health and social welfare programme of the country." Families would have access under this plan to information, facilities and services that will allow them the freedom to choose the number and spacing of their children. A National Population Council will be so established to implement this population policy and programme and to coordinate all the external aids and support for family planning throughout the country.

Like Nigeria, the Congo has retained virtually all of the population laws of the former colonial ruler – Belgium – which are pro-natalist in nature. President Mobutu is concerned with the problem of rapid urbanization, with the straining of education and health facilities and with the increasingly high rate of unemployment – all of these occurring despite the Congo's immense wealth in natural resources. Steps are therefore being considered to enunciate a national population policy which could more adequately harmonize the need for individual well-being with the need for the Congo's economic development.

Thus, both Nigeria and Kinchasa Congo are in the process of changing from the traditional pro-natalist policy to one which would take into account the country's resource-manpower relationship – economic development, on one hand, and respect for human rights and individual well-being, on the other.

Looking to the future, it must be observed that both of these factors, economic development and human rights, will undoubtedly help shape the legal change in Africa. If I were pushed to declare which of the two may assert the greater influence, I would be tempted to put human rights above economic development. With this in mind, one recent episode is quite revealing.

One of our consultants in the Law and Population Programme was recently asked to go to an African country and undertake a population project. This particular professor had been a legal advisor to that nation for about ten years and knew the country thoroughly. Upon arriving there, the local university, where he had also taught, invited him to address the law students. He chose, appropriately, to speak on the subject of family planning. He approached the topic from the viewpoint of economic development, arguing that uncontrolled population growth would tend to retard economic development. That argument, reasonable as it may have seemed, evoked extremely hostile reactions from the audience. Their counter-arguments were formulated like this: Africa, on the whole, is underpopulated in relation to its natural resources; in order to industrialize, to increase national income, there must be a sufficiently firm population base. Other students argued passionately that any attempt to sell population control or family planning to Africa would smack of white racism against the blacks.

A couple of months later, I had occasion to visit that same country, and was asked to give a presentation to the students while participating on a panel on the relationship between law and development. I also chose to speak about family planning. The Dean and members of the faculty were quite worried lest I fall victim to the same experience which my colleague had suffered. Nevertheless, I approached the subject from the point of view of human rights, arguing that family planning is a basic human right, a principle explicitly contained in the Tehran Proclamation on Human Rights in 1968. Since this particular proclamation was unanimously adopted, it meant that their own country had already accepted it.

I went on to indicate that if family planning is a basic human right, what then should be the law as to sales of contraceptives, as to dissemination of birth control information, as to public education – whether the process should include sex or human reproduction education? Furthermore, what should be the law regarding the minimum marriage age, public health, abortion, and sterilization? Indeed, could not one inquire further: what should be the laws relative to taxes, family allowances, inheritance, adoptions, social security, and land tenure?

What, you may ask, was the reaction of the students? They did not offer a single criticism or objection.

I could not help, of course, wondering about the differences in the reactions accorded to my colleague and me. My own guess is that it was in the name of human rights that the African nations obtained their independence. Under the banner of human rights they have opposed the apartheid in South Africa, opposed the Portuguese colonialism, opposed the events in Southern Rhodesia, opposed the British sale of arms to South Africa. Therefore, since family planning was now to be regarded as a human right, it was impossible for them to reject it. They could not ignore the basic right of family planning without compromising their basic positions of independence, equality and justice.

Herein perhaps lies a great potential or opportunity for family planning. And I will conclude with that rather optimistic note.

POPULATION LAW: NEW WINE IN NEW BOTTLES

*By David Tundermann**

I propose to shift our attention back to the domestic legal field and approach the subject of population law from an analytic – academic – perspective. Law schools in this country are now struggling with the question: what is population law. As Professor Wadlington has suggested, the question is not unlike the one raised three or four years ago when people were asking about poverty law. In formulating a course in poverty law one borrowed heavily from other recognized areas of the law, inserting parts of contract

*Student, Yale Law School; affiliated with The Population Council.

law, parts of property law – especially concentrating on landlord-tenant law – and parts of the law governing the treatment of welfare recipients, administrative law. Yet after this curricular innovation in poverty law, the years have indicated that the process has been circular. The segments of law pertinent to the study of poverty law are being reincorporated into the broader fields from which they were drawn.

The same kinds of potential problems may beset the law professors and students who wish to inquire whether there is a law of population. Perhaps the next few years will provide us with the answer. But I suspect that the full circle run by the poverty law fad will not be made with regard to population law, for the body of laws which influence population growth and distribution relates less to a particular economic class than did early compilations in the field of poverty law. If we define population law as the rules, the regulations and the procedures formulated by government institutions for the purpose of affecting population growth and distribution, perhaps that definition will describe a sufficiently focused field that will not fall apart with the passing of time.

Such a legal approach suggests a fairly complex matrix, encompassing many different kinds of laws that are now categorized in other groups of substantive laws. Perhaps the way to get a handle on a legal reclassification of rules would be to ask: what are the kinds of laws, legal institutions, and legal processes which influence the supply, as against the demand, for birth control products and services? This assumes that birth control activities are the touchstone, and rightly so. But beyond that we must ask, what are the kinds of legal processes that affect the supply and what are the kinds of legal processes that affect motivational factors?

This notion of supply and demand is useful for several reasons. First, it distinguishes mostly institutional delivery systems, that is, products delivery systems and medical delivery systems, from the complex motivational factors that are not adequately understood by behavioral scientists and legal sociologists at this point in time. Second, it permits us to put government law or program into its particular demographic perspective; for example, a family planning program becomes just one of a number of ways in which the availability of birth control products and services is increased or decreased. Mrs. Pilpel referred to many of the other kinds of legal structures – penal proscriptions, regulatory systems – that may also have an effect on the supply of birth control products and services. Indeed, they may directly contravene and frustrate the achievement of otherwise well-intentioned family planning programs.

In this general context several categories become evident. The first class is the complex of laws that affect the supply of fertility control products and services. This includes the penal statutes proscribing or restricting certain fertility planning activities; the common law principles of malpractice; and the state administrative schemes which actively regulate the availability of certain family planning services, like abortion, but defer to the medical profession the role regarding the availability of other kinds of family planning services, like sterilization. There are selective Federal interventions such as the FDA regulation of portions of the commercial market for contraceptives, and there are regulatory schemes which affect the availability of birth control products and services due to the impact on insurance programs.

The second category encompasses laws which affect demand. These are the legal processes which might affect the motivational determinants underlying the demand for birth control information and products. Since the allocation of child-care responsibilities among the individuals and the state may influence desires to have children, this category would include the law of domestic relations as it relates to child care. It would include the study of laws which delineate state and Federal subsidies for child-rearing expenses such as ADC and tax exemptions and deductions. And it would include the structure of inheritance laws which directly affect property distribution for child support purposes. Also included in the second category are the laws affecting the desirability of marital as against non-marital roles: laws prescribing requisites and consequences for marital dissolution, tax provisions favoring marital roles, civil rights, laws, selective service laws, and labor laws which relate to sexual discrimination and limit the opportunities for non-marital roles. In view of these laws, I would submit that men are affected just as are women.

Following this legal reclassification, which is no simple effort, an analytic approach is necessary to flush out, as it were, the many policies manifested in the laws affecting the supply and demand for birth control goods and services. It is important to determine, for example, whether or not a population policy has existed in the past, or if other policy objectives produce pro-natalist effects without the policy makers' knowledge.

This type of analysis has been performed by Professor Means in the *New York Law Forum.* He demonstrates through his investigation of the abortion laws that when supporting rationales decline over a period of time, it is important to re-examine laws which have a marked natalist effect and to ask, what are the social purposes served by them? If we consider demographic objectives as among the relevant considerations in the policy-making processes, how will the new balancing process turn out? Does the rationale underlying a scheme still hold true, or does it fall when re-examined in the light of changing demographic policies and social purposes.

Our objective is to examine the rationales which support the legal schemes that presently influence the supply and demand for birth control products and services, and, hence, begin to develop new theories, laws and institutional arrangements which will aid us in assessing the long-term consequences of the proposed fertility changes. I think the point here is that the incidence and the extent of birth control activities imply important consequences which are not presently given proper weight in the realm of public policy. New laws, new procedures, and new institutions are necessary to insure that the long-range consequences of fertility changes can be assessed and that the social costs and benefits can be weighed before widespread public projects are instituted which affect the supply and demand of birth control data. Lastly, I believe that initial development of new legal mechanisms for the expressed purpose of exploring all the consequences of a shift in population policy should be the goal of this new legal effort to analyze population law.

POPULATION POLICY AND LAW

*By Hugo Hoogenboom**

Editor's note: Though Mr. Hoogenboom was unable to attend the Symposium, his paper is included herein because it adds another dimension to the subject.

If people are beginning to think and talk about law and population – as distinct from the relationship of law to individuals – the discussion presumably rests on the assumption that societies must begin to adopt and implement population policies regarded as desirable or essential for the society, and that without these policies the aggregate result of individual behavior will be undesirable or disastrous for the societies involved.

There are three kinds of problems confronting policy makers. First, the best-known problem is rapid population growth in the developing world – regarded by most, but not all, economists and demographers as inhibiting rational economic development. Second, another widely discussed problem is the relatively lower, but still significant, population growth in the developed world, which is thought to pose ecological threats, to accelerate resource depletion, and to aggravate social problems generally. Third, and not as well-known, is the problem of too rapid a decline in fertility – regarded as threatening a diminution of national power (economic and military) as well as causing social problems. A fourth situation might be where there is no affirmative population policy but where policy is expressed by rejection of proposed laws that might influence fertility, for that very reason.

The kinds of laws that could be used to implement population policies and to solve population problems may be divided into three rough categories: 1) Laws directly affecting fertility by intervening at some point in the procreation process (through regulation of abortion, contraception, and sterilization); 2) Laws indirectly affecting fertility through regulation of social relationships related to fertility (marriage, descent and inheritance, sex status, etc.); 3) Laws indirectly affecting fertility through economic effects (tax, child allowances, maternity benefits).

Past experience may be a useful – though by no means the

***Regional Director, East and South Asia, The Population Council.**

only – guide to what role law may play in the implementation of population policy.

Population policies before World War II were primarily pro-natal. France, Germany, Italy, and Japan all attempted, by making fertility control difficult and by offering various kinds of incentives, to encourage people to marry and to have children. Typical measures included strict control of abortion and prohibitions against the sale, advertisement, and use of contraceptives on the one hand, and encouragement of fertility through child allowances, marriage loans, and other special incentives on the other. These policies were not very successful, if they were successful at all.

After World War II population policies were reversed, and so were the methods used to implement them. Contraception and sterilization were made freely available and people were encouraged to use them. In Japan, abortion was made legal. Various economic incentives and disincentives were proposed.

The reversal of population policies after World War II was dramatically illustrated in Japan. Concerned by the return of millions of overseas Japanese, a rising birthrate, in the setting of a ruined economy, Japan reconsidered its laws and policies. Abortion was liberalized in 1948, and became effectively available on demand in 1951. At the same time, contraception was also liberalized and ultimately officially encouraged (as a way to reduce the number of abortions), and the same laws making abortion available also liberalized sterilization. However, abortion became far and away the principal method of fertility control in Japan. Other factors were economic incentives inadvertently arising out of "pronatalist" requirements that companies had to pay family allowances based on numbers of children. This gave employment preference to people with fewer or no children – which may have had an anti-natalist effect – and may also have been the reason abortion was included in employee medical insurance coverage. (The cost of paying for abortions apparently also induced companies to open contraceptive clinics.)

To come full circle, Japan is once again considering a pronatalist policy. The Government, because Japan's net reproduction rate has been below replacement for the last ten years, asked its Population Problems Council to study the situation. An interim report was issued in 1969 which recommended that the Government consider adopting measures to ease the economic burden of having children, so as to bring the net reproduction rates back to replacement. No action appears to have been taken to implement this recommendation.

At first glance, it would appear that Japan provides an excellent case history of the use of law in implementing a population control program. However, the declining birth rate of the 1960's was probably simply a continuation of a trend that began in the 1900's which was merely interrupted in the 1940's.

Unfortunately, no other developed country has as yet adopted a deliberate anti-natalist policy, so Japan stands as the sole example. Probably, without the change in the law, it would have taken far longer for the trend in birth rate decline to reassert itself, so that we may argue that, even if it is not possible to induce radical change in behavior by law, it is at least possible to encourage and accelerate trends that already exist or have just begun. Legalization of abortion did this in Japan.

Underdeveloped countries began to become concerned about their rates of growth some time after Japan. India (where in 1930 the world's first government birth control clinic was established) adopted a population policy in 1952.

In Taiwan, the Provincial Government included a "pre-pregnancy health program" in its health activities from 1959 to 1962, and in 1962 it supported an experimental family planning program which by 1964 had been expanded to cover the whole island. An official policy was not adopted by the Government until 1968 – four years after the family planning program had become nationwide. Taiwan's annual population growth rate has fallen sharply and should reach 2.0 percent next year. Demographers argue whether this decline came about through the family planning program, because of economic and social development, or because of a high rate of (technically) illegal abortion. All three factors probably played a role. However, no legal changes were made in pursuit of either tacit or the explicit policy. The major change that has been proposed – but not yet enacted – is a law that would liberalize abortion and make sterilization legal.

It might be argued that land reform in Taiwan contributed to changing attitudes (although the reform took place quite a while before the decline in growth began). Unfortunately, no research has been done on this point.

Korea (South) adopted an official population policy in 1961

which, through two successive Five Year Plans, looked towards achieving an annual population increase rate of 2.0 percent by 1971 – a target which looks realistically achievable at this time. The one change made in Korean law in implementation of this policy was to repeal the old law prohibiting the importation of contraceptives. Korea now looks towards a third Five Year Plan (for the period 1972-1976) period during which a growth rate of 1.5 percent – or possibly 1.3 percent – will be the goal. Korea is generally regarded, together with Taiwan, as an exemplary case of a population policy implemented through a family planning program. Again, as with Taiwan, it can be argued that a large part of the decline in fertility Korea has experienced may well be attributable to economic development, social change (especially urbanization) and widely practiced though technically illegal abortion. Probably all factors contributed here.

The principal change in the law that has been proposed to date is a bill to liberalize abortion more or less on the Japanese model. The bill was introduced by the Korean Government last year, but was withdrawn in anticipation of this year's elections. The bill is expected to pass eventually, but no one seems willing to predict what effect it might have on fertility. The incidence of abortion in Korea is already extraordinarily high and seems to be rising, especially in rural areas. (For example, 20 percent of all 1969 pregnancies are estimated to have ended in abortion.)

As in Taiwan, there was a land reform, and it may be that this affected attitudes about the desirable number of children, but no research has been done on this point.

Thailand, which only last year adopted an official population policy supporting family planning as a means of combating the deleterious effects of rapid population growth, has already begun a nationwide family planning program providing contraceptive services and information through the existing health network. Even without public information campaigns or official funds, the program in Thailand has made considerable progress. There were 225,000 acceptors in 1970, compared to 122,000 in 1969. We expect numbers to go up again in 1971, and with the beginning of direct Government budgetary support in 1972 under the Five Year Plan, we expect the program to set growth rate targets, as happened in Taiwan and Korea. Thailand is unlike Korea and Taiwan since it is only on the verge of a successful implementation of its population policy. No laws needed to be changed to bring this situation about, and no changes have been proposed. Thailand does have a restrictive abortion law, but because of the Thai Buddhist ethic against taking life, it is more strictly interpreted by the medical profession than seems required. It is most unlikely that the law will be changed. Abortions are done illegally in Thailand by nonmedical persons.

Minimal legal changes have been made in other countries: Tunisia, Morocco, and Turkey, for example, repealed their anti-contraception laws; Tunisia also abolished polygamy (although it isn't clear what effect polygamy has on overall fertility), restricted children's allowances to the first four children, raised the age of marriage (to 17 for women and 20 for men), and permits abortion to requesting parents of five living children. Singapore has raised the price of delivery services in the Government-subsidized maternity hospital, has eliminated the requirement that all labor contracts provide for unlimited maternity leave (only three maternity leaves are required), and has stopped giving preference for public housing to families with children. India has stopped giving income tax exemptions for children or for wives.

In the range of legal actions taken or proposed seriously in the developing world, the legalization of contraceptives is certainly the most obvious step, since the alternative to contraception is rhythm, not a notoriously successful method. The next most obvious step would appear to be legalization of abortion. So far, no underdeveloped country has taken this step (although from the election returns, it appears that India may be the first). Indirect laws, such as changing the age of marriage, could have a profound impact, if they are thoroughly applied and enforced. Unfortunately, most indirect laws of this kind require some form of positive or negative action by the state to enforce them, which is troublesome in developing societies where inability to completely translate policy into action is a common characteristic. Enforcement is even more of a problem where a legal change goes directly against established custom. The more easily enforced indirect laws – the ones relating to taxation, child allowances, etc. – usually do not reach very far into developed societies. The people affected are usually the salaried urban classes, who are probably already limiting their fertility in any case. The bulk of the people in the developing world are little affected by the monetary economy, which is where laws regulating maternity benefits, child allowances, and so forth have their main effect.

So it seems that the law has played a secondary, rather technical role in the population policies of the developing world. The main thrust has been to change the law directly related to fertility, and, as a practical matter, only laws containing various prohibitions against contraceptives have been changed or repealed. Liberalization of abortion law has been proposed, unsuccessfully so far. There have been some efforts to affect fertility indirectly, but with what appears to be negligible – but certainly unmeasured – effect. Perhaps laws relating to land tenure and descent have exerted some influence, but there are no data.

Population policies in the developed world, where they exist at all, tend to be pro-natalist. In both Eastern and Western Europe, the law exists in a state of tension between pro-natalism on one side and individual freedom on the other. For example, in some Eastern European countries, the principle of freedom of abortion and contraception advocated by Lenin has been, to one degree or another, limited by official concern over declining growth rates, so that abortion is now severely restricted in Romania and limited in Bulgaria. Abortion was free in the Soviet Union after 1920, severely restricted again in 1936, and liberalized again in 1955. In France, despite the long-standing pro-natalist policy, the law prohibiting contraceptives was substantially liberalized in 1968.

The United States has no articulated population policy, although the President's Commission on Population Growth and the American Future will presumably remedy that. (The United States did at one time have a clear population policy of unlimited immigration). The laws regulating or prohibiting various methods of birth control were enacted, it seems, for reasons unrelated to population policy. Abortion was prohibited because it was medically unsafe, and contraception was outlawed as immoral. The struggle in the United States has been largely a jurisprudential one, seeking to establish individual freedom of control over procreation despite the law – and it remains to be seen whether the courts or the legislatures are to play the major role in liberalizing abortion in the United States.

The laws that seem to have had the profoundest impact on birth rates appear to have been those directly affecting control of procreation. The most dramatic cases are in abortion law. Japan, on the one hand, experienced a sharp decline in birth rates following abortion liberalization, and Romania, on the other, experienced a sharp rise in birth following a shift from a liberal to a severely restrictive abortion policy.

Removal or relaxation of laws restricting contraception in the developing world has had some effect, as in Korea, where that nation's successful family planning program could not have been mounted without repealing the old law.

The record seems to show that so far, policy makers have had the greatest impact on birth rates by changing the laws directly related to births. From a policy point of view, then, it would seem that first priority ought to be given to those laws. People concerned with using law as an instrument in advancing a population policy (pro- or anti-natalist) should look first at the laws regulating the availability of contraceptives. Laws to be inspected should include, in addition to those directly affecting sale, manufacture, advertisement, and distribution, such things as customs provisions and tax preferences. Policy makers should also look at the laws regulating abortion and sterilization.

Laws indirectly affecting fertility would require a great deal of careful consideration before being proposed. Because they are indirect, the effect of these laws on fertility is uncertain. At the same time, these laws also will affect other areas of public interest. Clearly, caution is required to avoid a situation where an indirect law has an undesirable social result in a nonfertility area while yielding a negligible result in fertility reduction (for example, sharp restriction on children's allowances after a certain number).

Laws indirectly affecting fertility are probably not worth a great deal of priority attention in most developing countries because there seems to be a lack of willingness to commit enough financial resources to direct programs, or to pursue them with sufficient vigor. After the straightforward problems facing population programs are overcome, then it may be useful to talk about indirection.

THE POLITICAL PROCESS AND LEGAL CHANGE

*By Thomas C. Lyons, Jr.**

I come to you as a political scientist, and I will share with you some of my feelings. And, I hope to identify some of my biases as I go along.

Politics, to me, encompasses the entire range of man's activities, directed at man's attempts to bring order and justice into his individual and his communal life. For better or worse, in sickness and in health, the political scientist and the lawyer are wedded, and professionally go through life together, concerned with this common goal. Not always, it seems to me, have we respectively done our job well, but the effort continues, and I applaud the John Bassett Moore Society for bringing this discussion about at this point in time.

As I said, I come as a political scientist, and I hope that means I come as a friend. And to prove it, I want to say right at the beginning that I do not agree with Shakespeare, who writes, in Henry VI, Part 2, Act 4, "The first thing we do, let's kill all the lawyers!" Nor do I accept H.L. Mencken's shattering dictum: that to every human problem there is a solution, all of them wrong!

What I propose to do tonight is to provide my legal brothers and sisters with some insights into the kinds of impediments that we can observe in the developing countries of the world, which may obstruct the legal change that would make population policy a viable political and social force. While perhaps my remarks would have been more appropriate to the first panel, I believe that there is legitimate reason to try and bridge the distance between the policy process and the legal change at this point in the Symposium.

> The time has already come when each country needs a considered national policy about what size of population, whether larger or smaller than at present, or the same, is most expedient. And having settled this problem, we must take steps to carry it into operation.

***Office of Population, Agency for International Development.**

This warning, contemporary in tone and intent, was actually uttered fifty-one years ago in 1920, by John Maynard Keynes. Twenty-five years later, in 1945, a leading American demographer of the time, Frank Lorrimer, wrote:

> The need for formulating and implementing realistic policies directed toward population control is both general and urgent.

In all the years since Plato, and here we are in 1971, there has emerged a relatively small body of literature on the aspects of population policy, and any serious discussions of policy have been limited to the most recent past. Obviously, what a government says and what it does need not coincide; and quite as obviously, what a country says and does may vary in tone and intent in as many directions and for as many reasons as there are countries, problems, religions, cultures and social mixtures.

A given country may believe it has too many people, but make no effort – or little effort – to affect the rate of growth. Another country may say it has no problem of excess people, but may in actuality support public birth control clinics. Another country may believe it is underpopulated, but offer family planning assistance based on a philosophical rather than a demographic ideal. Yet another country may believe that in terms of a steadily rising economic growth, its population is too small; but that in terms of an economic takeoff, it presently has too many people.

When, then, does a government acquire a policy? It may be unreasonable to say that a government has a policy only when it acts, for in fact, the inaction of another government may strongly imply a deliberate policy.

Since the early 1960's, when the connection between family planning and public policy began to be sensitized in this country, there has been a number of articles, monographs, conference papers and the like that have discussed in great detail the subject of national population-policy. But there have been few working definitions of such a policy.

Professor McCoy alerted us to the fact that we have gone until this afternoon, late in the afternoon, before anyone had attempted in a symposium dealing with population policy to identify what policy is. Let me share some thoughts on that with you.

Usually, it is assumed that everyone agrees on what population policy means, and population policy is usually used synonymously with programs. I have made a general review of the literature, to try and find a commonly accepted definition of population policy. My search included, but was not limited to, symposiums (international and national), monographs, papers, proceedings, textbooks, encyclopedias, Congressional records, and hearings and so forth, and I have concluded that population policy in everday usage lacks agreement on what constitutes that policy.

I offer a definition for your consideration.

> Population policy is a settled, determined or definite course, method or plan adopted and followed by legitimate organs of government, designed to reach and maintain a certain population growth and/or size.

Or, I offer this definition for your consideration:

> Population policy is a set of officially approved government activities and attitudes designed to promote the development of family planning services and the availability of contraception.

Now, these definitions have one serious drawback. Namely, they are so tightly constructed that perhaps with the exception of a few countries, almost no countries in the world would fit the definition. Perhaps it would be more realistic, albeit not as truthful, or accurate, to state that population growth limitation policy is "the government's implicit or explicit support of family planning activities by public or private organizations."

This more loosely constructed definition actually says nothing about achieving a demographic, social, economic, political or philosophical ideal, and further, the looser definition leaves out the consideration of officially approved and administered programs.

In the real world, a number of governments have decided to limit or decrease their population growth through the concept of voluntary fertility regulation. They do not all in the end, and at least at this point in time, have an all-encompassing, all-inclusive, integrated cross-sectional population policy. They support programs and policies with varying degrees of enthusiasm and commitment, some having set goals and others not. In a word, the diversity of policy in the less-developed countries is immense.

So that in the absence of an accepted – generally accepted – definition of policy, I offer the following criteria as a common denominator for those countries who have population policies.

First, there must be an official announcement of a population growth limitation policy; and second, some steps must have been taken to implement that policy. Those steps include not only the delivery of services through programs but also adjusting the forces of society in such a way as to assure the success of the goal the policy seeks to achieve.

In light of the overwhelming evidence that, one, rapid population growth in many less-developed countries carries with it the potential to disrupt the economic, political, social and ecological order, and two, the fact that a number of developed countries now are willing to help those who want to pursue population policies, and three, in spite of the fact that a number of developing countries – perhaps twenty or twenty-five – are pursuing policies designed to limit or halt their population growth, there are a number of people who raise the question: "Why have not more countries accepted a population policy?"

We now come to the point where I would like to ask you to crawl into the minds of the politicians in these countries, to see what it is, what kind of social, cultural, political forces, are brought to bear on the politician who must affect these policies.

I will identify these forces; I will not explain them, nor will I argue for or against them. I've observed these kinds of things in various countries of the world, and I list them under five major categories.

The first major category is that called nationalism – national pride.

Firstly, under that we find the following: that in spite of contrary evidence, population size and military strength is still positively correlated. The subliminal defense mechanism against national extinction dies hard. Secondly, we find that former colonial powers are associated with the advocacy of birth limitation. "White-country conspiracy" is heard sometimes. And thirdly, under national pride, we find elitist theories that postulate that lower classes would refuse family planning.

The second major category deals with the political or quasi-political impediments and constraints encountered in changing laws. This factor is simply called the fear of change.

Under fear of change, we find the following types of attitudes. First, poverty, illiteracy, and isolation create fatalism and inertia, resulting in governmental hesitation and contentment with the status quo. Such conditions work against change and feed the fear of cultural shock. And let's make no mistake about it; when you introduce a national family planning program, you are introducing change and in some cases cultural shock.

Second, under fear of change, we find the fear that traditional values will disappear and that unnecessary conflict will emerge from that family planning program. Third, some political leaders may be unsure of their administrative machinery, especially in situations requiring that machinery to take a lead in changing presently-held ideas. Fourth, given their understanding of social dynamics, some leaders believe their people will tolerate only a low level of innovation, imagination and experimentation. Fifth, they exhibit hesitation in starting country-wide national programs of an untested quality. Sixth, the knowledge that in one country where birth limitation was openly and intelligently pursued in a political environment of no apparent constraints and that government support of the program became an issue during the period of civil unrest deters government involvement in population control. And seventh, the fear that family planning is a sensitive issue with both the people and the formal and informal policy-approving elites.

The next major category is political. Under this category we find that politicians are reluctant to allocate for or mobilize a national program that has no apparent widespread public demand. Politicians and political leaders everywhere in the world are the same: they'd like to lend support to programs that show measurable results during their term of office. And the basic fact remains that results of population program efforts are not visible for a number of years. Third, family planning might be seen in the minds of some political leaders as inconsistent with cultural ideas of child labor, the role of women, and the dominance of males. Fourth, family planning and birth limitation is inconsistent with the personal behavior of important political and village elites. Fifth, the belief may be held that no developed country has achieved a low rate of population growth based upon a policy determination. Sixth, the urban areas that would attract the most successful family planning are also the seats of large non-nationalist minorities who aspire to more political and economic participation in their adopted countries. And further, these urban areas are the power bases of the government.

Seventh, some religious and political leaders are concerned if other religious and political groups are apathetic or non-responsive to birth control programs. Thus, in one state, in a large country, a majority religious group accounts for 91 percent of all sterilized persons with 82 percent of the population, and in a city in the same country, a religious minority group accounts for 20 percent of IUD insertions, but accounts for 13 percent of the population. These kinds of situations, when presented publicly and accusingly by opposing political leaders, give rise to political tensions many would wish to avoid.

Eighth, in some societies, religious-ethnic suspicion is replaced by tribal suspicion. For example, in one country where there are two large tribal groups, there are unsubstantiated rumors of population growth of one while the other tribe is decreasing its population through the use of the program. The fact that the rumors exist and are used, only intensifies political tension and clouds the efforts of the family planning programs.

And finally, in some countries, state or local politicians are uneasy about potential family planning success, in that if the local program is successful, they are likely to lose in the end because of immigrants looking for space, jobs and participation in a higher standard of living, and of reduced representation at the national level, if that participation is based on population size.

The fourth major category is that of economic policy, and under that you find the following. Some leaders, politicians, have an almost blind faith that the present economic policies are correct, and are therefore loathe to admit the need of family planning as a corrective measure. Moveover, the tension and pressure created by fast growth are believed necessary to force modernization, as demonstrated by the historical linkage between intellectual and economic advance in the Western nations, and population growth and social tension. Slower population growth may have a negative effect on economic growth, some say, at least in the long run, after the takeoff point has been achieved.

The last category is ideological; and under ideological, we find that intellectuals on both the left and the right, but especially in

Latin America, have lived a long time with the concept of underpopulation, not overpopulation. The orthodox Marxist believes that economic problems will be solved by socialism and nationalists believe that there is a huge continent to develop and populate.

In conclusion, I would like to share with you just a point or two about how I view the political and legal aspects as we try to make some sense out of these efforts.

Number One: I think that policy is the process whereby government reaction and action acquires legitimization and value.

Number Two: Policy development is oriented toward a sustained and stable political order, although tension and crisis give birth to policy as often as not.

Number Three: I think we have to realize that policy is never symmetrical. It is always complex, always dynamic, ever-changing, on-going; and I submit it is rational. It is the constant interplay between and among social forces, elite formations, political structure, cultural ethics, philosophical approaches, power relationships and so on.

Population policy and legal change are both important and difficult for the same reason. They both give official recognition and sanction to the problem and to its possible solution.

In the year to come, the desire on the part of governments to decrease fertility will continue to confront the desire of human beings to reproduce – a driving force in the history of civilization which is basic to human nature and is part of the laws governing life itself. Population policy and the body of law must reconcile the conflicting desire for reproduction with the absolute and sometimes immediate necessity for reduced fertility. The political and legal determinations will decide if, when and how this will be done.

POPULATION CONTROL BY CONSTITUTIONAL ANALOGUE

*By Cyril C. Means, Jr.**

I'm going to speak tonight about a little paradigm of problems of a Constitutional character in this country, which would accompany any serious efforts by either the state or the Federal government to apply coercive measures in the field of population policy. I published an article in the *Villanova Law Review* [1] last year which covers the subjects I will not discuss tonight. Those issues related principally to the question of where potentially coercive governmental power will be situated as pertaining to population control, and in the event that the Federal government be the actor, under our system of delegated power, what Constitutional precepts would justify such action.

What I short-changed in that article is what I would like to discuss tonight; something rather more basic and I think possibly of more general worldwide and less parochial American interest; namely, the specific nature of the right to reproduce, and whether there is any valid Constitutional analogue for the limitation, abridgement or regulation of such a right.

We all fear ghosts, and the ghosts that we as lawyers fear are dicta. So I shall commence by quoting you the two dicta, and as far as I've been able to determine there are no others, in the United States Supreme Court decisions regarding the right of procreation. The first is by Mr. Justice McReynolds in Meyer v. Nebraska, [2] decided in 1923, where he included under the penumbra of the Fourteenth Amendment's Due Process Clause, the right "to marry, establish a home and bring up children." [3]

*Professor, New York Law School.

1. Means, Constitutional Aspects of a National Population Policy, 15 Vill. L. Rev. 854 (1970).

2. 262 U.S. 390 (1923).

3. Id. at 399.

The other one is found in Skinner v. Oklahoma,[4] decided in 1942, where Mr. Justice Douglas referred to the right of procreation as one of the basic civil rights of man, and also as a basic liberty. These are pretty strong statements, and one might assume that the Justices were talking in absolute terms, about some thing that cannot be abridged by any authority under any circumstances.

Now, that is usually where a discussion ends when these dicta are referred to, but I would draw your attention to an analogous situation in regard to a First Amendment right of free speech, which is far more explicitly grounded in the words of the Constitutional text than is the right of reproduction.

These dicta do not say that the right of procreation is unlimited,do they? They don't say that there is a right to bring up an unlimited number of children. But we've always assumed that they meant that. Likewise, in regard to free speech I think we've always assumed that it meant the right to speak as many words as we pleased, and indeed, until the year 1920, it had always been understood to mean that no matter what the context.

However, I was reading a rather interesting article in the 1927 volume of the *Virginia Law Review*[5] not long ago called "The Radio Act of 1927." The author quoted from a message that Coolidge had sent to Congress which provided impetus for passage of this Act. And this is what the President had to say:

> Due to the decisions of the Courts, the authority of the Department [of Commerce] under the law of 1912 has broken down; many more stations have been operating than can be accommodated within the limited number of wavelengths available; further stations are in the course of construction; many stations have departed from the scheme of allocation set down by the Department, and the whole service of this most important public function has drifted into such chaos as seems likely, if not remedied, to destroy its great value.

4. 316 U.S. 535, 541 (1942).

5. W. Jefferson Davis, The Radio Act of 1927, 13 Va. L. Rev. 611 (1927).

> I most urgently recommend that this legislation should be speedily enacted. [6]

As a result of the President's recommendation, the Radio Act of 1927, which was the precursor of the Communications Act of 1934, now basically in effect, was indeed enacted.

Now, the Supreme Court did not get around to determining whether or not governmental allocation of this limited spectrum of radio wave lengths violated the First Amendment until 1943, when, in the case of NBC v. United States, [7] Mr. Justice Frankfurter, speaking for the Court, defined the issue and decided the question in these terms:

> We come finally to an appeal to the First Amendment. The Regulations, even if valid in all other respects, must fail because they abridge, say the appellants, their right of free speech. If that be so, it would follow that every person whose application for a license to operate a station is denied by the Commission is thereby denied his constitutional right of free speech. Freedom of utterance is abridged to many who wish to use the limited facilities of radio. Unlike other modes of expression, radio inherently is not available to all. That is its unique characteristic, and that is why, unlike other modes of expression, it is subject to governmental regulation. Because it cannot be used by all, some who wish to use it must be denied. But Congress did not authorize the Commission to choose among applicants upon the basis of their political, economic or social views, or upon any other capricious basis. [8]

And then he ends this famous passage by saying that the Congress did have power to define the terms of reference of the adminstrative agency, here the precursor of the FCC, by the formula of the "public interest" and he ends the peroration by saying that the standard for granting licenses to stations was

6. Id. at 612.

7. 319 U.S. 190 (1943).

8. Id. at 226.

the public interest, convenience, or necessity. "Denial of a station license on that ground, if valid under the Act, is not a denial of free speech." [9]

Now, lest any of you think that a decision as long ago as 1943, and one by Mr. Justice Frankfurter at that, is suspect of current Constitutional vitality, I should advise you to read the much more recent case of Red Lion Broadcasting Company v. FCC, [10] decided by the Supreme Court in 1969, where Mr. Justice White, speaking for the Court, reiterated in much smaller compass the Frankfurter reasoning, and then went on to say that:

> This has been the consistent view of the Court. Congress unquestionably has the power to grant and deny licenses and to eliminate existing stations.... No one has a First Amendment right to a license or to monopolize a radio frequency; to deny a station license because 'the public interest' requires it 'is not a denial of free speech.' [11]

Now, don't we have here valid analogue? Just as in times past the right to reproduce meant, because everyone understood it to mean, the right to reproduce without limitation, have we not now, in view of what all of the speakers have said, come at least in sight of a situation where, just as in the case of radio broadcasting, reproduction is now entering a new era – one in which there is a severe limitation upon the available resources of the planet, and therefore the reasoning of the radio cases, and of course now the television cases, would apply?

This is a sobering thought, because if it means that there would be set up another FCC which would perhaps be called the Fertility Control Commission, instead of the Federal Communications Commission, one immediately searches the mind for the more precise determinants of these rather vague guidelines of public convenience, interest, and necessity, which have been held to serve to authorize control in regard to the communications field. And yet I hardly think it possible to say that the right to reproduce one's kind is more sacred than the right to speak one's mind.

9. Id. at 227.

10. 395 U.S. 367 (1969).

11. Id. at 389.

Now, I simply suggest to you that, of course, there is a strong analogy here. And like all analogies, there are imperfections in it. In regard to human communication, of course, the traditional method is still available. If you want to speak unlimitedly, you have to do it on street corners or by buying a newspaper – something that's not quite as unlimited as it used to be. With regard to human reproduction – the population problem – the entire exercise has passed from the traditional unlimited sphere in which it always had been exercised into the sphere of limitation. Also, only a very small fraction of mankind is interested in communicating freely with his fellows, whereas a very large proportion of mankind is interested in reproducing.

Nevertheless, I suggest to you, even bearing these limitations in mind, that the analogy is valid – I shall not attempt to get into the controversy, if controversy it was, between my friend Harriet Pilpel and that indomitable, stormy petrel, Johnson Montgomery, because after all, they made up in the end anyway, and who am I to play the role of warmaker when peace has been declared? But in any case, I do feel that when we think of coercive measures, we must not merely think of one end of the spectrum, which is of course that vision of compulsory sterilization after two children which was conjured up by Mr. Justice Goldberg in his dictum in his concurring opinion in Griswold v. Connecticut.[12] We must also think of the other end of the spectrum, which isn't as coercive. Bills like Senator Packwood's[13] which would remove the tax exemption after the second child, or after some child somewhere along the line, and also like a bill[14] which has recently been introduced by my own Congressman, Representative Koch, which would eliminate the difference in taxation between married persons and single persons, are subtly coercive. And everywhere along the line between these two extremes one can imagine

12. 381 U.S. 479, 496-97 (1965).

13. S. 3632, 92d Cong., 1st Sess. (1971). The Packwood tax proposal has been subsequently defeated in committee. But Senator Packwood has since been working for the passage of a much more significant bill which would legalize abortion nationally. This bill, S. 1750, is now awaiting hearings before the Labor and Public Welfare Committee.

14. This proposed legislation, H.R. 850, is now languishing in the House Ways and Means Committee. The measure has 122 co-sponsors.

measures which certainly would be coercive in character, some more, some less.

I don't believe that these are subject to quite the same degree of Constitutional suspicion which the dicta that I commenced my address by reading you would indicate. I think that the reasoning of the radio cases would probably make such population control regulations valid.

CAN INTERNATIONAL LAW COPE WITH THE POPULATION CRISIS?

*By Ved P. Nanda**

If I could single out one conclusion after listening to the erudite remarks of the speakers thus far, it would be that the international dimensions of the problem are indeed overwhelming. I'd like to read from a statement by Doctor Phillip Handler, President of the National Academy of Sciences:

> Many of the most tragic ills of human existence find their origin in population growth. Hunger; pollution; crime; despoilation of the natural beauty of the planet; extermination of countless species of plants and animals; over-large, dirty, overcrowded cities, with their paradoxical loneliness; continual erosion of limited natural resources; and the seething unrest, which engenders the political instability that leads to [or might lead to] international conflicts and wars – all are derived from the unbridled growth of human populations.

You might take issue with this statement and suggest that there are many other factors besides overpopulation which cause these problems. But perhaps overpopulation remains the main issue. Many of you might have read the recent Pearson Commission

*Professor, University of Denver School of Law.

report, a report by the Commission on International Development, which was appointed by the World Bank, and headed by Lester Pearson, the distinguished Canadian statesman. This excellent report asserted that:

> No other phenomenon casts a darker shadow over the prospects for international development than the staggering growth of population. It is evident that it is a major cause of the large discrepancy between rates of economic improvement in rich and poor countries.

If the problem is acute, how aware are we of its serious nature? The general impression is that there is a growing awareness of the seriousness of the problem, but in a recent national poll, in answer to a question: "What do you think is the most important problem facing this country today?" less than 1 percent mentioned population. I believe the results would be similar in other parts of the world as well.

Today we've been discussing national family planning programs and policies. I think it would be advisable to evaluate national policies, no matter how you define those policies. I'd like to quote Robert McNamara, who has recently stated that if one were to candidly evaluate these policies, one would have to say that the national programs and policies have not been successful. He added: "With the exception of Singapore and Hong Kong, which are special cases, in only two developing countries, Taiwan and Korea, is there clear evidence that the rate of population growth has been significantly reduced by family planning programs."

If the projections on the future growth of world population are accurate, or even approximately accurate, the world population is supposed to reach beyond 6.5 billion by the year 2000, and the figure might even be closer to seven billion. And even if the "green revolution" will help us alleviate, at least for the time being, the problem of hunger and mass starvation which was earlier predicted to occur in the 1970's, there are other problems equally acute and serious, problems which are social, psychological and political in nature and have a bearing on the quality of life, such as problems pertaining to unemployment, housing, traffic, health, recreation, pollution, frustration, alienation, social stresses that might increase violence, crime, mental illness and suicide. If overpopulation could cause or perhaps aggravate these problems, and if the predictions are correct that many countries, especially developing countries, may not be able to curtail the high rate of population growth unless they take vigorous action and initiative now, then what are the alternatives? What can and should be done to take preventive steps?

I think all the speakers have taken a cautious approach in answering this question, obviously because they realize how sensitive this area is. All family planning and family assistance programs, whether they are under the auspices of the UN, private organizations or on a bilateral basis, are based on the premise that each country has a right to decide what its national population policy is going to be.

The sensitive nature of the subject matter can be illustrated by a recent UN action. You heard this afternoon that in April, 1970 the UN Economic and Social Council had adopted a resolution which called upon the Committee for the Second UN Development Decade, to include in its development strategy a reference to the high rate of population growth in some countries and the adverse consequences that might flow from such development. The pertinent part of the resolution read:

> In parts of the world, efforts during the Second United Nations Development Decade to promote long-term economic and social development adequate to improve the quality of life would be frustrated by the continuance of present high rates of population growth. In such cases, for countries which consider it appropriate and in accordance with the special needs of each country, national policies aimed at the achievement of more desirable rates of population growth and at the acceptance by parents on a voluntary basis of smaller families should be regarded as among the essential aspects of development strategy for the eventual achievement of satisfactory per capita economic growth, which would promote human welfare and dignity.

However the Committee did not accept this recommendation. Instead, it proposed that:

> Those developing countries which consider that their rate of population growth hampers their development will adopt measures which they deem necessary in accordance with their concept of development. Developed countries, consistent with their national policies, will upon request provide support through the supply of means for family planning and further research.

This Committee action was the result of the opposition by some states to the UN involvement in this area. Having said all that, and having listened along with you to other speakers addressing themselves to the programs on population undertaken thus far by the United Nations, the question occurs to me and it might have occurred to you too, as to the role of international law and international lawyers in controlling overpopulation. The first question obviously is: how relevant is Article 2(7) of the UN Charter in dealing with the population question? You recall that Article 2(7) does prohibit intervention in the internal affairs of nation-states; this prohibition is applicable to intervention by the United Nations and other international organizations as well. Does it mean that international law cannot deal with the issue? My answer would be that international law is relevant to the issue, it can deal with the problem, and it can be helpful in providing answers. For we should realize that in between the two extreme positions taken on this sensitive issue – one that there should be no international regulation whatsoever, and the other that compulsory and coercive measures should be taken to compel compliance with a world wide population strategy and policy – there are various shades of gray. Also, we should recognize that useful efforts can be made toward providing some kind of regional and international machinery, some norms, some guidelines which might induce, encourage, and assist states in controlling their rate of population growth.

First, I'd like to submit to you that a persuasive case can be made to support the thesis that the national population policies no longer lie exclusively within "domestic jurisdiction," that is they do not fall within the umbrella of Article 2(7).

There are at least three arguments in favor of the position I've just enunciated. First, it is a basic human right to have access to information and services on family planning which each state is obligated to provide to its citizens. The 1968 International Conference on Human Rights (The Tehran Conference) and the UN Human Rights program would support the contention.

Second, population pressures in a given state or region are likely to lead to internal disorder and political instability, which might affect or involve neighboring states or other outside powers in internal conflict and thereby endanger international peace and security. And third, the subject of population has now been transformed into a matter of international concern, just as in the 1960's the two issues of human rights, apartheid and colonialism, had become matters of international concern. The following events, among others, indicate that such transformation has taken place: (a) a majority of the 127 member states of the UN have officially favored and encouraged national, regional and international measures to lower fertility rates; (b) appeals for population control have been made by the UN Secretary General and the executive authorities of several UN agencies such as the World Bank, the FAO and the UNICEF; and (c) various UN organs and bodies have already undertaken active programs to assist family planning efforts.

However, even if the subject of population could be technically considered one of 'international concern', any contemplated international action would perhaps be opposed on ideological or religious grounds. It should be noted that although, until recently, both the communist states and several developing states were suspicious of the motives of predominantly Western states and organizations which were in the forefront of expressing concern over the rate of population growth in the developing states, the situation has dramatically changed in the last decade. The concern is now almost universal. It is becoming fashionable to discuss ways and means to control population. Also, notwithstanding the Papal Encyclical, the trend among Catholics is toward non-conformity with the Church dogma against the use of artificial birth control measures.

A second and equally important question pertains to the adoption of effective means to accomplish the goal of formulating and implementing a world population strategy. What seems to be absolutely essential at this stage is to establish a global population agency, headed by a UN High Commissioner on Population. This proposed agency should be closely related to a proposed global environmental agency. The Population agency should coordinate all current UN demographic and family planning research and assistance, set priorities, organize periodic world population conferences, and formulate a world population policy. Regional and national population agencies should be established to effectuate the global population strategy.

A final question remains: What measures would the population agency undertake and suggest to meet a situation when it determines that the population trend in a state is at considerable 'variance' from the set global policy? First, it should draw the attention of the state to the problem. Second, it should advise and encourage the state as to the nature and kind of measures the state should undertake. And finally, it should be willing to lend a helping hand by channelling the resources and expertise of specialized agents in assisting the state.

But what would happen if the state were unwilling to undertake even voluntary population control measures, or if such measures did not succeed? Should mandatory controls be imposed? If so,what would be the nature of these controls?

Also, should the World Bank, WHO and countries providing foreign aid use their aid programs as a leverage to bring about changes in the recipients' population policies? Perhaps at this stage donor countries and agencies should encourage the recipient country to formulate a population policy and provide information for dissemination but if active persuasion did not succeed, some control measures might have to be adopted. It might become necessary to recognize that parenthood is no longer a right but a privilege.

The nature of the control measures, if they are considered 'necessary', will obviously vary with the nature and gravity of the problem but the basic policy issue would remain constant in each case, that being the delicate balancing of the individual freedom versus the societal need.

I should conclude my remarks by suggesting that if population control measures are adopted in a state, it will be the lawyer's task to set reasonable standards and criteria, to provide appropriate checks and balances, and to institute the necessary judicial and extra-judicial procedures to protect the interests of the individual. Similarly, if such measures are adopted on an international scale, again it will be the lawyer whose task it will be to devise suitable machinery, set reasonable standards and provide adequate procedures to protect both the interests of the state and those of the individual. I do hope, as I am sure you do, that these control measures may never be needed.

Discussion

Professor Schwartz asked if any of the panel members would like to respond to anything said to this point.

Mr. Lyons raised two questions relative to what had transpired. The first raised the issue of the role of the male, which had distressed women participants. Why is all the emphasis on the female role? Perhaps it would be said that physical, biological differences are the cause. For a few hours a month women are fertile, whereas the male is potentially potent twenty-four hours a day. But what is really more to the point is the fact that the reduction of fertility in the demographic transition in the West took place before we had oral contraceptives, cervical devices, and IUD's. We are fairly certain that a decline began in the early stages of transition due to withdrawal and coitus interruptus; then later by the large scale application of the condom. In 1969, 15.5 million gross of condoms were sold in the world, to me that indicates that males are doing something to control fertility! Perhaps I am a male chauvinist pig, but I think that the point had to be made.

The second point concerns what is a basic human right. We must ask and answer the question: Where do these rights come from? Are they something we reach out and discover from time to time only to discover that they pass with history? Are they rights now but not rights in the future? Are they inalienable or do we just stumble onto them, as with constitutional and unconstitutional laws. These inquiries must be answered. Perhaps Dr. Lee, with whom I heartily agree, was correct in stating that population control programs and policy must be premised upon basic human rights rather than economic development. But I would again pose the questions: where do these rights come from; who discovered them; and what force do they have?

Dr. Ravenholt. The question of the origin of human rights, of course, is extremely difficult to nail down. I may say that it's part of the laws of nature, but then where does the law of nature come from? – from the Bible, from conscience, from man's reasoning?

Such an issue would take a long time to debate, and perhaps be rather inconclusive, but I would make this comment. We have often heard the argument that the universal Declaration of Human Rights to which, of course, the Tehran Proclamation on Human Rights is analogized, has no legally binding force. And consequently, it is only an expression of intent, a policy, hopefully to be fulfilled at some time. I myself feel, however, that this argument confuses the Declaration of Human Rights with human rights themselves. While the declaration may not be legally binding, human rights are. It has been rightly said human rights "are rights which attach to all human beings equally, whatever their nationalities," yet on the other hand we do hear such eminent scholars as Kelsen who insist that the Declaration of Human Rights has no legal effect, but I think we are talking about two different things. The Declaration, after all, was a product of the contemporary mortal beings; it was made in the context of the society at the time, reflecting the views of statesmen from different parts of the world; and I might add that the first Declaration is not infallible. The point is that human rights will remain forever, but the Declaration may be changed. Freedom from hunger, for example, was not explicitly contained in the Declaration, yet it was later embodied in the text. Family planning, too, was not explicitly mentioned in the original declaration, but yet it was later discovered and given world-wide acceptance. At the very least, human rights may be considered "general principles of law recognized by civilized nations." This, as all international lawyers would know, comes as the third source of international law in Article 38 of the World Court statute. Indeed, one might even say that these general principles have now assumed the character of customary international law; hence they are binding regardless of whether there is a convention or not.

Even the Declaration itself may have already approached the state of international law in the words of Dr. Edvard Hambro, the present President of the General Assembly, the Fifth Session:

> While the legal weight of the Declaration is not equal to that of a duly ratified convention, it does not mean that countries may violate its principles.
>
> The Declaration today carries greater weight than it did in 1948. During the intervening two decades it has entered into national constitutions, has inspired

legislation in a number of countries, has been quoted in judicial decisions, has been reaffirmed in Assembly resolutions, and has, of course, been frequently violated— what law or rule has not?

These violations have themselves been repeatedly denounced by the Assembly and in other reputable quarters. The fact is that the wide and pervasive international acceptance of the Declaration allows us to state that it has become, or that at least is becoming international law.

Professor Schwartz. The panel has indicated at this time a willingness and indeed an eagerness to entertain questions. I will remove the podium so that you can see the objects of your curiosity.

Question. If this problem of population explosion is as serious as has been presented today, and I believe it is as serious, why is it that our Federal government persists in giving tax exemptions directly proportionate to the size of the family? It seems that an inverse proportion would be much more appropriate to reduce this problem.

Mr. Lyons. Well, I think that you're assuming that a $625 exemption per child somehow influences the number of the children in the family.

Question. I'm not making that assumption, but it seems to me that for the family that has over, say two children, the equilibrium point, why would the government persist in giving them anything at all – no matter what the governmental interests are? Why would they give a $625 exemption to three, four or five children?

Mr. Lyons. There are probably historical reasons. We were not faced with the population problem at the time that the law was formulated. But on the other hand, we have to stop and ask, if the government had a no-tax exemption for children at all, whether or not this would affect the children, and I think there is good reason to suspect that it would.

Dr. Ravenholt felt that the government followed a very simple principle in that it gives an exemption for every person. It happens that those persons come in various sizes and clusters, but that does not deny to any of them the fact that each is a person.

Mrs. Pilpel added that maybe it has something to do with the fact that there are many people who have no control over their fertility, and therefore it would seem quite unfair to penalize them in any way until we are satisfied that they could prevent having more children if they wanted to.

Professor Schwartz. Please go to the mike and identify yourself if you wish to become important TV personages.

Mr. Kerr Nash, of the Population Commission, observed that as a political scientist, he was enamored of the easy way in which Professor Means created power. But on the other hand – and perhaps he was being cautious among lawyers – he still felt a bit uneasy because it seems too facile. Specifically, he had four brief points to raise. The first was in regard to the question of coercion; what's coercive and what's not coercive. It seemed to him that when we run so quickly from the mandatory pill or whatever to the Packwood proposal, there is perhaps more difficult territory to cover along the way. He argued that Professor Means did not deal adequately with the difficulties. It seems that perhaps in this regard, there is an easier Constitutional argument, to the effect that if the government wishes to neutralize – whatever "neutralize" may be – it is perfectly clear that the present tax structure, or the present structure of what we call hidden policies in terms of say population distribution, is not neutral. It is clearly, on balance, pro-natalist. It would seem to me a good bit easier to get to a point of neutrality under the Constitution than to suggest that there is no difficulty in reversing the tax exemptions, or start cutting them down. One sub-point was made: what about the effective date of such a change? Is this a bit analogous to some of those court decisions about retroactivity? Perhaps the age-cohort structure will be distorted and the birth rate will be increased prior to the policy change. Such changes always involve unknown difficulties.

The second point had to do with Means' analogue. Again, the simplistic approach was objected to as it strained to meet the point. The regulation of the number of radio channels can hardly be compared to the potential regulation of birth rates. There's a clear distinction between the obvious finites of the spectrum of radio waves and the much less proximate finites of this world as a justification for restrictive action under the Constitution.

The third point related to what the Supreme Court has recently been doing. An analysis of Griswold or Belous, the California decision, reveals that both were in effect creating a kind of absolute right, sort of laissez-faire right in the woman to do what she wants with her body in terms of having children; that there's a kind of unconscious analogy there, between what those courts have been doing in the last few years and what the Supreme Court was doing in regard to the businessmen and laissez-faire rights between approximately the late 1880's and 1937, when the switch occurred. Does – pardon the pun – the recent course of adjudication on this issue, look like fertile ground for a switch in course, thus enabling the government to say: "No, the woman doesn't have this right."

The final point was an extension of Mr. Lyons' point; that has to do with the political problems of applying these sanctions. One major difficulty is that it is going to stabilize the proportions between different ethnic groups; that is politically unfeasible in the 1970's.

Professor Means. Now, on the question of what is coercion and what is not, I suppose it depends upon how you define it, or where you draw the line. Clearly, the compulsory sterilization after two children, which Mr. Justice Goldberg mentioned in the dicta in his concurring opinion in the Griswold case, would be defined as compulsory.

Now, as to an economic benefit withheld or granted, a bounty for doing what the state wants or an economic penalty for doing what the state doesn't want, if moderate in size, probably most people would say it was not coercive. On the other hand, the Population Council has had to consider what the effect might be of offering a man the equivalent of a whole year's wages for doing something. Wouldn't this amount to such a tremendous offer that it could possibly reach the point of coercion? The courts traditionally have defined coercion in fairly physical terms. The Goldberg dictum is coercion; the Packwood arrangement or the Koch arrangement would not be. But to venture a guess as to where the Court would draw the line would be to indulge in foolhardy speculation.

I will jump to Mr. Nash's third question about the laissez-faire that seems to be recognized in the woman, under the Belous decision and under the Griswold decision, if one can call that conjuries of fragmented opinions a decision. The Belous case can at least be understood because it's a clear majority, speaking in an integrated text. I think Mr. Nash has a point there. I've always been very unhappy about that particular form of reasoning. If Mr. Justice Peters of the Supreme Court of California had said the right of the woman to limit her reproduction or the right of the woman to choose not to bear a child, that's really all he had to say, because that's the only thing that was involved in the case; trying to broaden it out, giving a little something to everybody by saying to decide whether or not to bear a child was dicta causes me to object as I do to the language in the Tehran Declaration. Incidentally, I have been informed only tonight that the reason the Tehran form of the Declaration was adopted as it was was to secure the concurrence of the Holy See. Obviously, those of us who have been active in the abortion liberalization movement as well as in the legislative proposal, or in an effort to obtain Constitutional declarations of invalidity of the anti-abortion laws, have only felt it necessary to emphasize the asserted right of the woman to refuse to bear a child.

I take quite seriously my analogue of the radio stations and the airwaves, and the Radio Act of 1927, and its successor legislation, has not said that each one of the 200 million Americans has got a right to one-two hundred millionth of the spectrum of the airways. It says that there is a Commission set up which shall choose who shall have a manageable fragment of this spectrum. It seems likely that this will in the end turn out to be the case with regard to human reproduction, some commission will have to choose certain people and say: "These are the ones that are going to beget and bear the children, and all others are excluded from the exercise of that license." Now obviously, capricious and arbitrary distinctions based upon race, creed, color and all the other paraphenalia we're used to would not be permissible in that as in any other governmental activity; it is not permissible in regard to the radio waves. The very point of the Red Lion case was to affirm, and the Supreme Court did there affirm, the fairness doctrine which the Commission itself had developed over many, many years.

As to Mr. Nash's second point, I find it most difficult to

answer, and that's why I put it off to the end. He rightly says that there was simply no difference of opinion in the public between the years 1920 when the question first arose and the year 1927 when the Radio Act was passed, that there was a limited spectrum of radio waves. Everybody knew it; everybody knew you couldn't have 90 million all sharing equally. There, people simply accepted these realities and in fact the word reality occurs in the Court's opinions on this subject. I suppose one would have to be insane to ignore those realities. I don't think we can say that about the question of over-population; I think there's a growing consensus that over-population is here, or is just around the corner; if we are willing to halve our standard of living, we can probably double our population. That would not be reality. So there are variables here that were not present in the rather clear-cut scientific case of the radio spectrum. Nevertheless, I think that it's a valid analogy, and I would simply add your point to one of the others, that analogies are not perfect.

Mr. Montgomery. I represent Zero Population Growth; I would like to amplify the answer to the last question and then pose another question based on that answer. In Griswold v. Connecticut, Mr. Justice Goldberg said:

> Surely a government, absent a compelling, subordinating state interest, could not sterilize a husband and wife after they had borne two children.

The implication of that remark is that if we did have a compelling, subordinating state interest, perhaps we could have compulsory sterilization after two children or three, or whatever. Incidentally, that language was quoted in the Belous decision and in Mr. Justice Douglas' decision for the Court in the Griswold case; there is other language which shows that what we're doing here is balancing the needs of the society against the desires, the needs and the human rights of individuals. Now the question is: how serious, actually, is this population crisis, and what kind of implications can we draw from this analysis by our domestic courts in the international community?

It is considerably easy for our domestic courts to come along two or three years from now and find the compelling, subordinating state interest which would warrant governmental population control. And whatever method the Congress thinks is needed will be provided for. But we can't do that in international law. We can't sit in the United Nations and coerce the world. Now, how does that difference in analysis lead us to any realistic solution to the worldwide population problem?

Professor Nanda. I don't believe that we can take the domestic law analogies and apply them in the international law arena. It simply can't be done. I do feel that the way to create the necessary international legal regime is to create a kind of consensus through the declarations by multinational organizations. We can probably use diplomacy; we can use ideological strategy; we can use dissemination of information; we can use what's being called voluntary measures, but I am skeptical about the utility of this voluntarism; perhaps it might become necessary to use mandatory courses.

Mr. Robert Goldman. I would like in that regard to flag one issue which I think has perhaps emerged but has not been clearly articulated. I think that international lawyers sometimes take a view of law which has almost resulted from the institutional limitation. We have heard a good deal of confidence expressed in our ability to develop a useful international consensus through declarations in lawmaking which take the form of advance statements. I think that Professor Means' suggestion of a commission, domestically, indicates that on any level we indulge in a very difficult balancing of interests test. Here, we have a decision which is profoundly political, in the sense that we are going to have to reconcile important interests; to believe that those interests can be reconciled with any degree of precision in the United Nations Charter or in a constitution is, I think, to delude ourselves. What is really needed is the kind of institution in which we are prepared to repose some degree of confidence, which suggests that the importance of the Supreme Court is not so much that we have a written constitution but the fact that we have an acceptable reason for having a place of last resort, on questions to which we can't really find the answers in the text or the history of the Constitution. Neither can we find the answer to questions of international law in the text or history of the United Nations Charter. The terrible problem is: we do not have either a Supreme Court or a Congress operating to answer these questions with any degree of particularity in the international sphere. I do think, however, it's unfortunate to place one's hopes in verbalized declarations of principle, when we're down to hard questions of stepping on some toes, in order to accomplish certain objectives.

A point that Professor Nanda made toward the end of his talk, which I thought was particularly interesting, in view of the fact that most of the conference has been devoted to a description of policies and objectives, and very little has been done towards actual implementation in terms of target states, was the Article 2(7) discussion he mentioned. Certainly it's no secret that in the past, the World Bank group, and indeed, the United States, has exercised considerable leverage on the determination of internal economic development in monetary policies of developing states. This may be characterized as Machiavellian. But in view of the continuing dependence of the developing world on external financial assistance, as is evidenced in the Pearson and the recent credit reports, why cannot the international community, through the World Bank group – particularly the World Bank and the IMF, together with AID – merely perform a *fait accompli*, and say, as a precondition for aid, that nations must undertake birth control policies? In other words, make birth control a matter of international concern, much as fixed stable unitary exchange rates are now?

Professor Nanda. Family planning: that's a promising prospect; that's a beginning. But the issue still would be that these international agencies, loans and projects in developing countries are not going to affect the multitude of the populace. Yet at the present time, as you know, aid programs do apply leverage. I think that leverage is going to be used in the future, but I don't feel that that's going to be an ultimate answer, and therefore I'll rely on my earlier assertion that perhaps the answer lies in the dissemination of information.

Mr. Lyons. I feel that probably nothing would serve to destroy the foreign aid program more than to set this kind of condition to the acquisition of aid. Moreover, I think the political repercussions around the world, were it ever to be debated openly, would be serious indeed.

Mr. Goldman. The only reason why I'd possibly dispute that is that there is evidence and we do know, despite what Mr. Schweitzer may tell us, and what Mr. McNamara will tell us, that conditions of internal financial stability, for instance, that loans, standby loans, by the IMF, are constantly denied to nations, especially in Latin America, and other developing states which pursue economic development policies, for instance, which entail inflation, payments and balances, or have quantitative restrictions on trade and development. Now, certainly these things slap at the sovereignty of nations, and Mr. Schweitzer and his group in Washington, in many cases, have been determining the development policy of nations like Argentina and Uruguay and Brazil for a good number of years. In many cases, we do know that when these loans have been denied, that AID and other private bank resources in this country and abroad have been upheld. Now, if these are matters of concern, certainly development is the most important thing to these nations, and if these nations do know what the score is in that regard, to impose a precondition of population control would be of no consequence. In other words, we've already interfered substantially with the development process; would it be so awful to continue?

But you still stand by your statement?

Mr. Lyons. Well, I think such a policy would be severe; indeed it would. I think there's nothing wrong with requiring the economic development planning board in each country to crank into all their calculations the demographic equation. But it's another thing to say: "Now, you must do what we tell you to do about it." That is the difference, and the World Bank itself requires that all economic studies and applications for loans show that in the planning that goes on, whether it's sectoral or cross-country planning, that the population problem has at least been looked at by the economists, the planners, and other administrative officials.

Dr. Ravenholt. Our experience to date would indicate that this matter of tying development assistance to the population program issues is not necessary, provided the population program assistance is made avaliable as grant assistance. Initially, we had a great deal of difficulty, because of the long heritage of loan assistance, and i-a number of countries where loans were tried, as a means of assistance for family planning activities, nothing effective happened. In fact, such loans obstructed further effective action. But where grants of dollar or commodity assistance were made available in appropriate fashion to many countries, there has not really been a lack of takers; they are being accepted and used quite quickly. Where the World Bank is in difficulty is that it can only provide loan assistance, rather than grant assistance, and this is indeed a problem.

Professor Means. I'd like to make just one point about the course that the dialogue has taken in the last few minutes. I think it's premised upon the unspoken supposition that the developed country that is extending the grant or making the loan is in a position to adopt a high moralistic attitude in dealing with the developing country, in saying that the recipient country is over-populating, that it has to do something about it in order to benefit by our largesse. Now, this attitude has been around for some time; it's aroused a good deal of resentment on the part of the recipients of these bits of largesse, and I think that it is probably factually founded, because we now know that the developed countries, because of their much higher rate of consumption of resources and their much higher rate of pollution of the environment per capita, do, by a much smaller birth rate, or increase rate, enough of their own so that they're not in quite the position to adopt this high moralistic tone. Consequently, the thought occurred to me that perhaps a very useful sphere of international agreement could be aimed at if we could get some kind of international body set up which would determine quantitatively what the pollution index and rate of consumption of natural resources index per capita was for each country of the world. And then get them all to sit down and say: "All right, now we multiply that times our population, and then we agree, each of us, to limit our population to the extent necessary in order to make an overall across-the-board reduction of this general amount of unpleasantness that we're all producing." Now clearly, the developing nations are producing unpleasantness through having too many people, more than through pollution and natural resources; we're developing unpleasantness in the developed countries by overpolluting and overconsuming. But nevertheless, by reducing the whole thing and making the reduction in the reproduction rate, or the net increase rate depend on a factor of this kind, I think one would be in a position to achieve a considerably greater degree of international accord on this subject.

Whereupon the panel was adjourned.

REPORT OF TASK FORCES AND GENERAL DISCUSSION

QUESTIONS CONSIDERED BY THE TASK FORCES

TASK FORCE I. What changes, if any, in U.S. foreign policy regarding population control would you recommend for the 1970's?

What is the distinction between the problems of the developed countries and the less developed countries in this area? For example, are population control efforts likely to be effective in the absence of real economic and social development? What should the priorities be, given the many problems and limited resources? Should the United States concentrate on building roads or on population control in its foreign aid program? Regarding U.S. population control efforts, should the U.S. attach conditions to the use of its aid in this area?

TASK FORCE II. What should be the appropriate role, in the population area, of (a) private organizations, (b) governmental organizations, and (c) international organizations, especially the United Nations?

TASK FORCE III. Is "family planning" a human right? What is meant by a human right in this regard: access to information and/or birth control devices for all? Can this right be legislated? Does family planning as a human right negate the possibility of coercive laws in the population area?

Each task force spent half its time on the questions specifically assigned to it and the remainder of its time divided between the questions assigned to the other two task forces.

REPORT OF TASK FORCE I

Mr. William Serow*: While the U.S. should not slow up its supply of contraceptive services, it should pay more attention to dissemination and availability of services, possibly through improved use of commercial channels.

Hitherto, policy has been oriented to availability of contraceptives, rather than usage. However, steps should be taken to augment usage as well. U.S. policy should become more oriented to the needs of recipient nations and to individual consumers within those nations.

In terms of program organizations, there was a consensus that agencies active in foreign policy should coordinate their efforts. For example, the United States Information Agency might distribute film and other material on family planning in the United States to demonstrate that the U.S. is actively putting into practice the advice it gives other nations. It was also pointed out that presently the United States Public Health Service is not easily able to render assistance outside the United States.

The role of private organizations is a rather special one. They are frequently able to develop more imaginative programs, since they do not operate under the restraint of controls and governmental agencies. Frequently they are able to give support and initiative and even opposition to government programs. The relative free hand they're able to operate with enables them to develop different sorts of programs in different places than government agencies are able to.

***Assistant Director, Office of Population and Economics, University of Virginia.**

Many programs of United Nations agencies are under way; many of these are fairly new but showing encouraging signs of progress. A few agencies have fallen seriously behind in some of their assigned tasks. It was felt that these agencies are unable to do their job, and the assigned tasks should be relegated to other more competent agencies.

One area where it was felt that international agencies could have considerable impact was that of easing problems of redundant research efforts. It appears that it would be most beneficial if there were one agency to coordinate research efforts and to insure that inputs into world polls of knowledge would be available to all.

It was agreed that the right to have as many or as few children as desired is a basic human right. The right of having the desired number of children at the desired interval should be guaranteed, but it must be emphasized that with every right there goes a duty.

Cultural change within the framework of a given society may be necessary to insure this freedom of choice. The fact that one's forebearers may have had ten children is no reason for an individual to have to do so. At the same time the guaranteed freedom of choice implies that the actions of one individual do not impair those of another. Consequently, making decisions as to the number of children and the spacing of these children is a cost and benefit to the society as a whole, as well as the individual, which must be considered in the quest for socio-economic development.

REPORT OF TASK FORCE II

Dr. Miriam Birdwhistell*: Our group did not try to make a group statement on Item Number 3. We did not have time to speak about it; we spent more than two hours talking as rapidly as we could on the question itemized under Number 2. We felt that Number 3 was certainly important and complex, and that's the reason we hesitated to make any statement. One member did suggest that we state and emphasize that family planning is a right rather than a social responsibility.

Our experts in the Task Force seem to have ample evidence that women all over the world want to control their reproduction,

*Faculty member, University of Virginia Medical School.

but this must be balanced against national governments' fears that the developed countries will try to force them to limit populations.

Mrs. Oyekunle, of Nigeria, emphasized the fact that population problems cannot be separated out or attacked separately from other social and economic problems. She felt that free and compulsory education, women's rights, training for employment other than domestic work, availability of employment and alternative roles to motherhood should be supplied for women. This was a theme that ran through the entire two and a half hours of discussion: the population problem should not be attacked on a unilateral basis, but attacked simultaneously with these other socio-economic problems. This approach, seen also in our recommendations regarding structural arrangements, is the only one that will be acceptable to under-developed nations and which would allay their suspicions that the developed nations have an ulterior power-access motive in lowered population.

As Dr. Ravenholt, who was in our task force, said over and over about women all over the world, they will use contraceptive devices whenever we can get to them. So we're not faced with whether the demand is there, whether there is a market, but we are faced with securing the most perfect technology and delivery systems for making it known and available, preferably without cost. In order to illustrate that women will go to any limits to avoid reproduction, Dr. Ravenholt pointed out that many women will even go into debt just to pay for an abortion. The preventive program we seek will be one that makes reproduction control available for each woman no matter where she lives.

We considered recommending adding to Article 16 of the United Nations Declaration of Rights, to speak specifically of a girl's right to have a period of maturing physically, socially, economically, and educationally after puberty and through adolescence before she enters reproduction, and even then a girl should have a choice as to whether she enters reproduction at all.

The UN Declaration statements speak of the right of women at full age to found a family. Well, the term "full age" is a compromise, not to offend any of the signatory nations. Sometimes it means to one of them puberty, to another it means twenty-one. Therefore, this was used so they could all agree on full age.

But the Declaration has not been ratified by these same countries, so in addition to being vague, it does not have effect. Any more elaboration of rights via this route, for our task force, is futile.

Our task force then approached the structural problem. In order to promote the attack on population problems, described as one aspect of social and economic upgrading, we see the present structures we have as providing an adequate framework. We recommend no proliferation of organizational formats at this time.

On an international level we have both government agencies and private agencies. With government agencies funneling more money into private agencies such as International Planned Parenthood, they can give very good service in education and disseminating information, and will improve, as the experts tell us.

On the national and local levels also, international private agencies should be able to look for coordination of cross-functions to the international governmental agencies.

On an international level, the UN is the goal we look to. We think of the developing nations' role as necessarily moving, and quickly, to multilateral organizational help through the UN and bilateral functions to be phased out as quickly as possible. Our expert, Dr. Ravenholt, tells us this is a goal of his agency, of course, AID, as always, and that it will happen quickly. Our task force, including him, believes AID aid to the UN can be stepped up and should, to the ten-percent level, from its present five percent of the total AID program.

Direct delivery of family planning assistance to other national governments of developing countries will be through international agencies. The UN should be the coordinating body for all population problems. The fairly recently created UN Fund for Population Action, a semi-autonomous funding body now, should exert leadership for all units of the UN specialized agencies so that they would incorporate the population problem as an integrated part of their attacking other problems, such as agriculture, public health, education. This UN Fund should not usurp any of these agencies' specific areas, but it, if it sees that they are inflexible and not doing the job, should contract out for services elsewhere, or in some way spearhead attacking the problem at hand.

The World Bank as an international organization should also make more useful population loans and encourage population control activities in conjunction with loans in other areas, such as education.

It was emphasized that national governments, with all access to persuasive information and knowledge of the available loans in many areas, should develop their own integrated approach to the population problem, but that each one should be thought of on a case-by-case basis, and different packages of both national and international help should be put together to suit each country's particular situation.

REPORT OF TASK FORCE III

Mr. Geoffrey Keppel*: I'm the student rapporteur on Task Force III. My job will be to talk about the differences of opinion on Task Force III. And then the Chairman, Mrs. Biggar, will come and pour oil over troubled waters.

I felt it was a most stimulating task force and there was a wide range of opinion. We dealt exclusively with the questions: "Is family planning a human right? What is meant by 'human right' in this regard? Access to information or birth control devices for all? Can this right be legislated? Does family planning as a human right negate the possibility of coercive laws in the population area?"

It was in this last area where we got into a most heated kind of debate. Mr. Lyons from AID put it in a very good equation. I don't know if the audience can read it, so I'm going to read it for the audience. "Responsible parenthood culturally defined" – culturally defined because obviously we're dealing with a highly complex and worldwide problem, parenthood in Nigeria and America are two different things – "is a basic human duty." Underneath it is, "Equal opportunity to control individual fertility is a basic human right." And at first Mr. Lyons had this equalling "Freedom is a basic human necessity," but at lunch he changed the equal sign to an arrow and the word "necessity" to "goal." Of course we know that if freedom is a human necessity, it doesn't exist in a lot of areas of the world; so we changed this to an arrow pointing at "Freedom is a basic human goal." Taking that as the starting point, we began to look at family planning as a two-tiered thing. It is both a right and a duty. There were differences on what the right to family planning is. Is the right just

*Second year student, University of Virginia School of Law.

to have access to birth control information and contraceptive devices, or would the right extend to perhaps having in this country a much more intensive sort of public education campaign, so that people were actually made aware of the population problem and the availability of fertility control devices?

Mrs. Harriet Pilpel basically, and perhaps I'm being unfair to her, wanted to end the debate there. She said, "This is the essential task facing this country, that voluntarism has not been given a chance." No one really knows, or at least in many areas of this country, especially among poor people, about the ability to control fertility.

But there were some of us on the task force that wanted to take up this second question, which is the one above here. Responsible parenthood is a basic human duty. Mr. Montgomery wrote out a statement which I put in brackets there – I guess the audience won't be able to read this, so I will. The first of these four provisos is actually a contribution by Mr. Shaw, who is a distinguished lawyer participating on the task force. The first proviso is: "There is a basic human right for family planning;" the second is: "providing no person shall exercise this right by having more children than he can responsibly care for and educate." Third: "providing each person shall have equal right to have wanted children." And fourth, "provided, finally, that all humans combined do not have more children than all the world's resources can support on a sustained basis."

Mr. Montgomery's basic position, and I may be unfair to him at this point, is that our society is moving at such a rapid rate in terms of its problems and of the population explosion that a coercive law limiting each family to two children should come into effect. Dr. Freymann's point of view was that, well, there's a weakening of the genetic pool already, and that things just don't operate that way. It would probably be better to let some women have four or five children and others not have any at all. He has given me a rather sophisticated analysis and extension of that observation which I hope he will give this session later on.

Mrs. Pilpel wanted the Symposium to focus on voluntarism and what can be done in this country in terms of making these devices and information available to every family in the United States. Now, some of these are tall orders already, because in terms of an advertising campaign, for example, who's going to give us the money to go to Madison Avenue and start advertising, say, the advantages of family planning. We don't have this money, and I don't think any of the various organizations in the field have the money right now to mount such an advertising campaign. And I doubt if we can get the money from General Motors, because they need people to buy their cars.

Then the other side: some of us were saying that really you don't just want to look at voluntarism and its potential, because events are moving too quickly in our country. The problems are telescoping themselves at a rapid rate, and that you've got to start thinking about coercion.

But if you start thinking about coercion, and the possibility that maybe it is going to be upon us unless we do reorder our priorities and do get money for example into the ghetto area so that the population there can perhaps be reduced – not population, but unwanted children, the possibility of unwanted children can be reduced – you get into a more activist frame of mind.

There were many on the task force that did not want to even talk about coercive laws, and then there were some of us who did. And again, the reason why is that we think the population problems are growing at a much more rapid rate than perhaps, say, Mrs. Pilpel, who has been in this field for a long time, can appreciate. She has been looking at the problem since the 1930's when voluntarism in this country was not allowed. But now the problem has gotten to the point where the available resources in the world are being depleted at an alarming rate, and the population of the world is still – I guess here you have to allow for differences of opinion – is still increasing at a fairly alarming rate. We were given statistics on that yesterday. So maybe our only alternative is to leapfrog voluntarism and go to coercive laws.

I think those are the basic divisions in Task Force III. And they weren't really resolved by the end of the meeting.

Now I'll call on Mrs. Biggar to perhaps tell us that there was a lot more agreement.

COMMENT

Mrs. Jeanne C. Biggar*: The real debate we will not be able to settle. But before we leave Task Force III, it did seem to me there

***Acting Assistant Professor, Department of Sociology and Anthropology, University of Virginia.**

were at least some principles on which there was agreement. And this was agreement to at least three types of human rights, although each member in this task force agreed that this was a difficult concept to pin down. I think it can be said that we agree that every woman has an equal right to information and to services for the termination of pregnancy, or for the prevention of pregnancy.

Secondly, that every family has the right to at least limit the size of the family. But what we could not agree on was whether we were talking about only limiting or controlling the size of the family. And the third point of agreement in this group was that every child has a right to: one expressed it as "tender, loving care," another said, "to nurture and the proper education in the light of his own culture."

The second question that we were challenged with, we simply did not address, the question as to whether this right could be legislated. We particularly did not address it in terms of the international realm. And it was the third question, "Does family planning as a human right negate the possibility of coercive laws in the population area?" that we found difficult to come to agreement on.

Some of the members believed it must be redefined in terms of, "Will family planning negate the possibility?"

One segment of us insisted that moving to the level of coercion in fact served as a divergence from our consideration of what we can do to implement existing programs. The other segment of us felt that we must, in fact, move to some consideration of coercive laws.

One statement given at the close of the task force, however, I think is a statement that we could all agree on. All persons in a human group have the right and the need for means whereby childbearing patterns, which under prevailing conditions, if we could define this, are optimal for individual and group welfare, can be considered and effectively promoted, preserving to the maximum extent, individual liberty and opportunity for variation.

We realized at the close of our period that in fact we had permitted ourselves to consider only two extremes – that of a passive voluntarism position and that of a coercive position. We have not given proper consideration to the many degrees in between, and as Geoffrey reminded us, Doctor Freymann, at that point in time pointed out that family planning as it exists at the present time is not a passive program, that it's an educating and emancipating and promoting program, which permits families to rationally consider the alternatives they have in the area of bearing children.

DISCUSSION

Mr. James Rummonds*. Thank you all for the enlightening presentation of what transpired at each of your workshops. I think that certainly gives us a large area to start picking into.

We went through basically three areas, it appears. One was the first group, which was looking for policy in the broad context of what this country might do to effect change in the area of fertility planning in the developed and underdeveloped countries. The second task force went through and looked at the role that might be played by various institutions, both in this country and abroad, and private institutions. The third task force dealt mainly with the problem of rights.

Now, from this point onwards, we'd like to take any questions that any of you have regarding the issues that were brought up by the workshop rapporteurs or chairmen, and we'd like to come to some kind of fundamental consensus about, at least, what was said in each of these areas, so the findings of each of the groups might be clearly presented to us.

Are there any questions?

Professor McCoy. I have a question in the nature of dissent with the second task force, of which I was a member. It has to do with the issue of attitudes and the demand for family planning services. It was my understanding, and it's still my belief, that one of the crucial tasks which remains in the population field is the question of attitudes, cultural norms, behavior patterns, which very significantly limit family planning services, and if I'm not incorrect, I believe that our chairman indicated that this was not a problem.

*Third year student, Stanford University School of Law. Here acting as chairman of the general discussion.

Mrs. Pilpel. I'm not sure it was made clear by Mr. Keppel that proviso number one was not assented to by most of the people in the workshop. I myself opposed it on the ground that the last part of it, "more children than he can responsibly care for and educate," perpetuated some sort of a status quo which many of us thought was improper. And I believe Mr. Shaw finally withdrew that word on the ground that it was too conclusive, and we all concurred that no person could emphasize the right – that every person had a right to have only wanted children.

In other words, I think one is out. Second of all, even if I have talked too much about voluntarism, I just want to state for the record that I consider voluntarism a very active program, and that if I have any major criticism of those who talked about coercion, it is not that they are more active, but that they are more passive. We voluntarists are in favor of actively working toward repeal of the laws, we're in favor of actively promulgating an educational campaign. We're in favor of actively doing everything that can be done so that people will be able to exercise their right of freedom of choice, including the making available of the supplies, services and information which we think the government has an obligation to make available.

So, although it's true we didn't touch on that until the end, I think it is plain that all people who believe in voluntarism believe in a very active kind of activism.

Mr. Shaw. Mr. Chairman, my name is Bradford Shaw, and I was a member of the third task force. Mrs. Pilpel, for whom I have the greatest respect and whom I contradict with considerable concern, has said that I withdrew the parenthetical phrase in paragraph one, stated on the board.

Rather than withdrawing it, my suggestion was that we add to it "within the opportunities available within his own culture."

Mr. Rummonds. So we want to add to number one up here, "within the opporunities available within his own culture."

Mr. Shaw. That's right. That is, rather than withdrawing the phrase as a whole.

Mr. Rummonds. "Providing no person shall exercise this right by having more children than he can responsibly care for and educate within the opportunities provided by his own culture."

Professor Caldwell. I should like to comment upon three distinct aspects of this discussion. The first relates to whether human rights can be legislated. It is quite clear that in many areas the legal system can require, permit, or prohibit discrete activities in ways that either deny or give substance to an alleged human right. For example, in the pursuit of our goals in population planning, we can require sex education in the schools, and the creation of public family planning clinics with services available to all persons without regard to ability to pay. We can also enact a great deal of permissive legislation freeing individual citizens to perform antinatilist activities theretofore proscribed by law. Finally, we can adopt laws that forbid, under civil or criminal penalty, action that is essentially pronatalist. A comprehensive survey of the entire legal structure in any society will reveal the various ways in which contract, tort, criminal, property, and tax laws, for example, interlock in the support of a policy that may or may not be consonant with an articulated human right. The major task is to identify the "right" and then examine ways by which the normative structure can be modified in terms of rights, permissions, and prohibitions to support that right. In this connection, it would have been helpful to have the inputs from experts in domestic relations law. Two separate trends in that field have contradictory import for the future of our population policy. One is represented by the movement to take away the legal and social stigma of illegitimacy; the other is connected with women's liberation. A recent example is the case of a single woman in the armed forces who insisted on retaining her job and the custody of her illegitimate child, presumably in the best interests both of the mother and the child. I believe that it is not necessarily the case that the feminists' program will be wholly antinatalist in effect. Will child care centers enable mothers to substitute the joys of the job for motherhood, or will they merely make motherhood and career economically and emotionally so satisfying that child care facilities actually operate as a further incentive for reproduction in order to attain the best of both worlds?

With reference to a second issue, I regret that we do not have among our experts several cultural anthropologists and psychologists to emphasize a point that has been raised by our visitors from other countries, namely, that high fertility, especially in the production of male heirs, is deeply imbedded in the structure of self-esteem among many foreign cultures. Garcia Lorca made the point in his poem, *Yerma,* dramatizing the anguish of the young wife who believed that she was sterile. In such cultures, the efficacy, safety, and availability of technological means for regulating fertility are wholly irrelevant.

My third point concerns the very real possibility that the President's Commission on Population Policy will recommend the creation of a Presidential Advisory Council on Population Policy – parallel to the National Commission on Enviornmental Policy – with a mandate to federal agencies to consider and estimate the potential population impacts (numbers and distribution) of every measure or program that may be suggested at the federal level. It might have been appropriate for this group of experts to consider what body of persons, with what kinds of skills and techniques, could possible fill the departmental posts demanded by such a mandate. We are far behind in the development of a sophisticated framework of analysis for grappling with the kinds of questions that would emerge from such legislation. Perhaps the next regional meeting can focus upon that issue: how can we advise legislative and executive authority about probable population impacts of proposed legislation and governmental programs.

Professor Fitzgerald of the Law School at the University of Louisville. I'd just like to add one footnote to what has already been said about the discussions that took place in Task Force III. One of the things that I've been most fascinated by in this conference, and I think it was overlooked in the report of this task force, is the question of the relationship between family planning and control of consumption, or economic reform.

Many of the foreign students, both yesterday and in Task Force III this morning, indicated that they did not believe we could talk about a basic human right to family planning, or at least talk about any of the international implications, whether we're talking about international law or international cooperation, or trans-national cooperation, as some of the speakers preferred to think might be more feasible, apart from some kind of international cooperation or discussion of the control of consumption. This is one thing I think should definitely have been mentioned by Task Force III.

The only other thing I would add as a footnote to Mary Ellen's comments a moment ago about the absence of sociologists and psychologists, I think that when you're talking about questions like basic human rights, which have ethical or moral implications, that you're short-sighted when you do not include in your study and in your discussions, ethnicists and moralists as well as the people represented here. This is another interdisciplinary area that needs a great deal more consideration than has been given to it in this conference.

Dr. Lee. I think we want to add a further caution against the assumption that a right to information on family planning, if implemented, will solve most of the problems in regard to overpopulation. In the first place, available evidence does not support this argument. To give an example, Taiwan has sufficient evidence to show that even now, a majority of women will not come for family planning until after she has been visited by the field worker as often as four or five times. This in itself would raise a number of interesting questions.

First, does it mean these women are already past, shall we say, their impressionable school years; consequently, they need a little bit more persuasion than otherwise would have been the case if they had been in school? Second, what are the capabilities of most countries, especially countries with huge populations – will they have the manpower and financial resources and so on to enable the field worker to visit each woman four or five times?

And finally, what is the difference between the freedom of planning, on one hand, and here, where you have four or five visits, approaching a kind of coercion, which we discussed in our task force? But these are just questions I throw out.

Mr. Rummonds. I think it's very important also to remember that such concepts as freedom, responsibility, duties of individuals are generally defined by culture and by the dominant institutions within each of these cultures. I'd hate to see us all accept freedom as being something that exists solely within the definition that western countries tend to put it in.

Mrs. Fitzgerald of Louisville, Kentucky. There's one problem which I see that has not been mentioned very many times in the whole conference. We are not specifically concerned with it, but there are some individuals in this room who are concerned with it.

Very little has been said here about the kind of birth control devices and methods which are now available. Many women feel that the devices that are now on the market, are now available, are unsatisfactory or unsafe. Some people feel that they really are dangerous to a woman's health, and/or are not practical. Even the prostaglandins, which Dr. Ravenholt thinks will solve our problems, are not going to be applauded by a large group of women who simply do not agree with abortion. And I think a group like this must continue to encourage the scientific world to – not to stop and not to pat themselves on the back because they have the birth control pill or some other kind of device. It seems to me that the only thing that the scientific world cannot do now is to provide women with a good, safe, effective conception control device.

Mr. Keppel. I'd like to be a little bit provocative for a minute. We've had a fairly good symposium, but perhaps because of the nature of symposia, something that I've been disappointed in is that we haven't really looked at this population problem in its totality. Dr. Luke T. Lee talked about the difficulty of getting Taiwanese women to go to family planning centers, and yet Dr. Ravenholt says that women are dying to get contraceptive devices around the world!

Dr. Ravenholt. I said they were dying because they weren't getting them.

Mr. Keppel. But in any case, I think that there are other problems that I'd just sort of like to throw out in a kind of provocative way, that I see involved in the population problem. Take the role of the United States government and its foreign policy. The country of Brazil seems to be an expansionist country now; certainly in its population policy, it is extremely pronatalistic. It's taken an extreme position in the United Nations to date on this issue. Now why? Well, it's got a military government now in power, and maybe Brazil sees itself as the continental power in South America. Part of the problem is that the United States government helped the Brazilian government get where it is today. Now, this problem hasn't been discussed at this symposium. There are very honorable, hard-working men in AID who are trying to get into Brazil and trying to persuade Brazil to not take a pronatalist policy. And yet Brazil has it now. What kind of a dialogue is going on between the Pentagon and between the population office of AID on this kind of a question? Let me just frame that question for Mr. Claxton.

Mr. Claxton. I think the simple answer is that there is no dialogue between the AID and the Pentagon on the subject right now, and I think with reasons that should be apparent to you. There are enough difficulties surrounding the whole problem of trying to encourage the developing countries to even understand the population problem and work with it, and the implications for them on the kind of action they should take on it, without involving any kind of military implication. To involve the Pentagon, to involve the CIA would simply give some additional force to those people in the developing countries who are suspicious of our motives.

Dr. Cordovez of Ecuador. I would like to raise another point of view. This is the point of view of Latin American countries that believe, backed up by many activities and scientific studies, that one of the means for achievement of an economic development would be getting more population and distributing this population to undeveloped areas, where there are enormous resources for people to develop. Economists are discussing this and they haven't agreed on the matter. It is something the United States did, that is, encouraging immigrants and settlers to populate and develop its open spaces.

Mr. Rummonds. I think that if you'd ask a few American Indians what they thought about that policy, they'd disagree strongly on what the economists advocate.

Mr. Dalzell from the University of North Carolina at Chapel Hill. The statement on the board about the basic right to family planning raises three questions in my mind, and it may be because I don't understand the words.

There are three provisos. The first one, "provided no person shall exercise the basic right by having more children than he can responsibly care for and educate, in accordance with the culture," presumes, I suppose, that before the person has any children, he knows how many children he can educate. I think there's some question about that, although that doesn't raise nearly as much question in my mind as the second and third provisos.

The second is "provided each person shall have equal right to have wanted children." Does that mean that every person can have as many children as he wants? That's what it seems to me to mean. I'd like to have that explained.

And the last leaves me completely floored, "provided, finally, that all humans combined shall not have more children than all the world's resources can support on a sustained basis." That transfers the right of the individual marriage to the rights of everybody in the whole world. I don't see how that's possible to resolve.

Mr. Chang from Taiwan, Republic of China. I would like to raise another point of cultural background which may undermine family planning, in response to Dr. Lee's point. In China, and of course in some other Oriental countries, it is true that it is a great humiliation for the wife who doesn't have any sons, only daughters, because the Chinese old people are always taken care of by their sons, but not their daughters.

In some cases, the wives may have had five or six daughters, but they don't have any sons, so they are making efforts to have a son, even one son is enough. Maybe we can make a differentiation from the words son or daughter in Chinese. In Taiwan, we say "son" is "hausay." It means "effective birth." We say a "daughter" is "solokyang." This means just "daughter."

So daughter is not an effective birth. It's rather ridiculous, but this is true. So in some developing countries education – in other words, how to persuade the family to have a correct idea of family planning – I think is much more important than simply giving them the means.

Mencius, our great saint – he is next to Confucius – said that it is a man's greatest disloyalty to his family if he doesn't have any sons. And this idea still influences our family very much.

Mr. Aklog Birara of Ethiopia. I have several criticisms of the whole proceeding. One, there has really been a lack of definition as to what this kind of proceeding is seeking to achieve. I think we would have time to define the population growth problem and the difficulties in terms of distribution of resources while setting a standard. We're sort of saying, "The world's population cannot be supported by the resources available." But by what standard? What is subsistence? Is it having two motorcars, a television set, a radio, a house, three children? You know, the American dream.

Two, we haven't mentioned the fact that there should be an assessment of redistribution of resources. The world is divided into haves and have-nots. And the haves are those who have technological advancement and who are consumers. Therefore, in any assessment, in any rational analysis of the population growth, we need to redefine how we can redistribute resources so that people don't have too much to consume, while others don't have anything to subsist on. An American consumes about 50 or 60 times more than a native in India. Therefore, isn't it also necessary for us to reach a conclusion that there needs to be a lessening of conspicuous consumption on the part of developed countries?

Another point is the unwillingness of developed countries to take the initiative, or even to be willing to contribute, say, what was set by the United Nations, that is one percent of the GNP to the United Nations for the development of less developed countries. There hasn't been really that initiative, with the exception of a few countries like Sweden. There hasn't been the contribution of one percent to the development of developing countries. One of the greatest obstacles to raising the standard of living of different countries in Asia, the Middle East, and even Latin America, is that they lack the diffusion of technology – i.e., by that I mean, the need for capital-producing goods. We need also to analyze the need to diffuse technology to the several countries, so that we can eliminate the dependency of developing countries towards developed countries.

A final point, and then I will quit. The final point that I really want to bring up is this. In policy making the assumption on the part of the United States, AID and other agencies, is not to interfere in the sovereignty of the countries. But the difficulty in the past has been that while some small aid was given to developing countries, say, like Kenya, or Ethiopia, or Ghana, or Taiwan, there hasn't been a very daring, radical approach to sensitizing, is the word, I think, the leadership of these countries to bring about agrarian reforms. Eighty-five percent of the people in the third world, in many countries, do not own land. So how can we expect the reduction of birth rates when at the same time we know that there is no utilization of the land? Maybe this is something that we need to think about when we go back and formulate policies. And therefore I would end my monologue this way: That in any sensitive discussion of population growth, in terms of the developing countries, there has to be a sensible, sensitive, and rather dynamic analysis of the economic forces within these countries as a whole; a comparative, rational analysis of the specific negative aspects of population growth, the need for economic reform, and the need for rational utilization of aid.

Mr. Odujinrin of Nigeria. Very much has been said about AID, but I wonder whether what is given is aid indeed. After all, you are supposed to use whatever is given in aid to buy from developed countries, and at inflated rates. In 1964 it was suggested that the developed countries should grant preferences to the industrial products of the LDC's. At that time the United States said, granting preferences to the LDC's would not help, and that, granting preferences to the LDC's would be discriminating against the developed countries. But one wonders whether this is so, in view of the fact that the developing countries and the LDC's are not equal. It is sensible to discriminate in favor of the weaker party over the stronger party. The federal government gives aid, or what is called "adjustment assistance" to the weaker parts of industry. So if the government can give aid to these weaker industries in order to compete favorably with GM and other industries, why not discriminate in favor of the less developed countries?

Mr. Keough. It's also important for America that the Pearson Report pointed out that the most serious problem for the social and economic development of the developing countries is rapid population growth. So that if you tie the two things together, it is not one against the other. It's not that you have a one percent and ignore the serious problems created by the kind of population growth in the development of the world – forty percent of the population being under fifteen and so on, therefore having to have all kinds of consumption expenditures, which prevent capital formation, to support the people.

There are two blades to consider here. You do need both, the education, the information, the awareness of the implications, both economic and social – and human – of population growth, and the awareness of the different problems in different countries. Brazil may present different kinds of issues than Costa Rica or the Far East and Middle East. But there are certain common features, and one of those common features is that rapid population growth does make it more and more difficult to achieve the objectives of each of the countries that have accepted social and economic development as their goal. I think one of the things that came out of the discussions in Task Force II – I'm sorry I wasn't here when it was summarized, but I think it's important – is that one of the serious problems is to somehow break the point between puberty and reproduction, so that there is a greater time lapse. And the suggestion made was not to raise the recommendation

Whereupon the Symposium was adjourned.

SELECTED PAPERS

POPULATION CONTROL IN INDIA: SOME SOCIO-LEGAL ASPECTS

*By Clarence T. Dias**

There has certainly been no dearth of Jeremiahs making gloomy prognostications about the effectiveness of the programs adopted in India for the control of population expansion. India's family planning programs have attracted a generous amount of scholarly scrutiny and critical appraisal. But most of the existing studies of population control in India have tended to suffer from the same preoccupation with the modalities of population limitation that characterize the very programs themselves. Such preoccupation with the modalities, while entirely understandable, is nonetheless rather unfortunate in that it has diverted attention from some of the broader sociological issues underlying them and from consideration of the role of the legal system in facing up to those issues. This note represents an attempt to raise (with a degree of generality) some of those issues and also to focus with some particularity on two possible modalities of population control in an effort to indicate the role that law and lawyers might play in the field. An attempt will be made to briefly examine the role of legal rules and institutions in inducing, in conjunction with a series of other political drives, a climate of social acceptance which will increase the effectiveness of programs for population control in India.

Two Specific Modalities

Two proposals aimed at helping reduce the country's fertility are receiving the consideration of the Indian Parliament. These proposals are in the form of bills to raise the minimum age at marriage for females and to liberalize abortion.

A study based on published census data shows that the mean age of women at marriage has increased from 12.6 in the 1921-31

***University of Bombay, Department of Law**

decade to 15.5 in the 1941-51 decade, while that of men has remained more or less stationary at twenty.[1] The increase of roughly three years in the age of women at marriage within a period of 20 years would, on rough calculation, result in a three per cent decline in the birth rate.[2] Marrying at a higher age does cut down the reproductive span. Moreover, it is an established fact that either as a result of being generally more mature, or because of greater opportunities for education and for gainful employment, or a combination of these, girls marrying at a later age favor and adopt family planning more readily.[3] Recent studies indicate that if the minimum age at marriage for females were fixed at twenty years the reduction in the birth rate in a decade would range from 12 to 30 percent.[4] In any event, there appears to exist a distinct correlation between raising the marriage age of females and reducing the country's birth rate. The Child Marriage Restraint Act of 1929 fixed the minimum age at marriage for females at 14. This figure was raised to 15 in the year 1957. Non-compliance with the provisions of this statute gives rise to criminal liability. In addition to this statute there are numerous other provisions of domestic relations law in India which appertain to the age at marriage. It may be pointed out that in India several systems of personal laws co-exist. Depending upon one's religion one could be governed by the Hindu Marriage Act, Mohammedan law, the Indian Christian Marriage Act, or the Parsi Marriage and Divorce Act. In addition there also exists the secular Special Marriage Act which is primarily applicable to marriages between spouses practicing different religions. Such law also prescribes a minimum age at marriage and this age varies from one personal law system to another. Under the Special Marriage Act the female must have completed the age of eighteen years at the time of the marriage otherwise the marriage is a nullity. Under the Hindu Marriage Act, the bride must have completed the age of 15 years and moreover, if she is between the ages of 15 and 18 the consent of her parents or guardian must be obtained for the marriage. Non-compliance with this provision leads to curious

1. Agarwala, "The Age of Marriage in India," 23 Population Index 96 (1957).
2. Agarwala, "Population Control in India: Progress and Prospects," 24 Law and Contemporary Problems 577, at 580 (1960).
3. Chandrasekhar, "How India Is Tackling Her Population Problem," 13 Population Review 28, at 34 (1969).
4. Id.

results thanks to the quixotic and eccentric nature of the drafting of the statute.

Where the bride is between the ages of 15 and 18 years and her parents' consent is obtained "by force or fraud" then the marriage is voidable at the bride's option. But due to a lacuna in the statute, where such parental consent is just not obtained at all, the marriage remains valid nonetheless. Further, non-compliance with the age limit of 15 years presented by the statute does not invalidate the marriage but merely gives rise to criminal liability.[5] Under Mohammedan law any person who has attained puberty has capacity to contract a marriage and further a minor girl can be given in marriage by her father or her guardian. Of course, if the girl is below 15 years of age the provisions of the criminal statute – the Child Restraint Marriage Act – will be attracted but the validity of the marriage remains unimpaired.[6]

Before turning to some legal arguments as regards the question of raising of the marriage age, it would be pertinent to briefly mention some of the sociological issues raised by such a move, since legislation on so sensitive a subject as this might lead to surprising side effects and the cure might prove to be worse than the malady.[7] Studies would need to be undertaken examining carefully the psycho-sexual impact of such a move upon women. In a society like India, where women traditionally marry at an early age, raising this age to twenty will cause a major change in life styles and an articulation of fresh societal demands. In urban areas the probable result of raising the marriage age for women could be a trend towards more women going in for college education and possibly an increasing influx of women into professional fields. This would be a desirable trend to establish. In rural areas, however, it is difficult to envisage what results will flow from the raising of the marriage age. Moreover, even though the marriage age for males is not proposed to be raised, still the

5. The person procuring the marriage of a girl below the age of 15 is punishable with imprisonment which may extend up to 15 days or with a fine which may extend to one thousand rupees (which is approximately the equivalent of $134.00) or both.

6. One need not here consider the provision of the Parsi and Christian law because they are basically similar to the types of legislation already described.

7. For a brilliant exposition of exactly such being the case in Russia see Massell, "Law as an Instrument of Revolutionary Change in a Traditional Milieu," 2 Law and Society Review 179 (1968).

raising of the age for women could have effects on the male in view of the strong prejudice prevailing in India against marrying an older woman. This might, at first glance, seem to work very much in favor of lowering the fertility because it would tend to foster later marriages for even the male who would tend not to marry before reaching 20 years of age, if that were the minimum age set for the female. But whether such delayed marriages will lead to a decrease in the birth rate or to an increase in the number of illegitimate births will depend upon at least two factors: the attitude of the society towards premarital sex in general and prostitution in particular and the use that is made of section 488 of the Criminal Procedure Code. The said section provides a summary procedure whereby the Court can order a person to provide maintenance for his wife or his legitimate or illegitimate child. Depending upon the attitude that Courts take as regards the stringency of proof of paternity, this section could assume enormous effectiveness as a deterrent against having illegitimate children. Moreover, such a deterrent would have a much sounder sociological basis than the traditional deterrent which springs from the social stigma attached to illegitimacy. Whereas such stigma attaches to the child, the deterrent in section 488 of the Criminal Procedure Code operates directly against the putative father. The issues raised above regarding the raising of the marriage age for females are issues that sociologists would probably be more competent to handle than lawyers.

Let us now turn to some legal issues. Assuming that it is desirable to raise the marriage age for females to 20 years, it would then be the task of the lawyer to come up with provisions attempting to implement this and to evolve legal rules which will be honored more through compliance than breach. With this in mind perhaps it would not be enough just to raise the age to 20 years in the criminal statute – the Child Marriage Restraint Act. Perhaps it would be desirable to also amend the marriage laws and seek a uniform rule whereby non-compliance with the age requirement will render the marriage null and void. Practice has shown this to be a more effective sanction than mere criminal punishment. At any event, one of the tasks that lawyers should address themselves to is the reform of marriage laws (such as the provision of the Hindu Marriage Act referred to earlier) which at the moment are clearly failing to effectuate the policies they were designed for.

Section 312 of the Indian Penal Code[8] makes it illegal to induce any abortion except "in good faith for the purpose of saving the life of the woman." The punishment for violation of this section is almost Draconian and could extend to imprisonment for a term of up to seven years. A bill proposing to legalize abortions is pending before the Indian Parliament. Supporters of the bill would point to sociological and psychological literature to show that unwanted children grow up in unhappy homes and often experience childhood traumas which lead them to become delinquents and a threat to law and order. In any event, a reasonably strong case can be made, purely on medical grounds, for the legalization of abortions. One has only to turn to instances of butchery perpetrated by quacks to meet several of the ethical arguments often advanced against legalizing abortions. For India, one of the main questions that needs to be resolved is whether legalizing abortion will so overstrain the Indian medical profession as to extend it virtually to breaking point. Studies would indicate that the medical profession in India would be well equipped to cope with the added responsibilities such a move would bring.[9]

Another aspect which needs to be carefully studied is whether an abortion causes significant psychological damage to the woman. Kinsey's study of the sexual behavior of the American female shows that 9 per cent of the women reported a certain degree of psychological disturbance following abortion. It seems likely that the attitudes of the women are the result of social mores more than individual volition. Thus, if both society and the law approve of induced abortion, a woman's trauma after an abortion will be considerably lessened. The lawyer's role as regards this mode of population control seems relatively restricted. All that would be needed would be repeal of the existing criminal law regarding abortion. One might also suggest the establishment of "abortion

8. The Indian criminal code, unlike codes in the United States, is a federal statute and applies uniformly in all Indian states and to people of all religious persuasions.

9. See for example B. Krishna Rao, "The Impact of Legislation of Induced Abortion," 45 Journal of the Indian Medical Association 97 (1965). Moreover, Soviet scientists have prepared an aborting device on the suction principle which is virtually harmless and which does not need special surgical supervision during the operation which lasts no more than five minutes.

clinics" through which abortions are to be handled almost exclusively. This would enable involvement of social workers and psychiatric personnel to ensure the minimization of the psychological effects of an abortion. It would also enable the state to keep control and supervision over the abortions performed.

Conclusion

Any large-scale family planning program has to take into consideration short-term as well as long-term objectives. Measures which are undertaken in order to reduce the birth rate as quickly as possible have to be chosen carefully so as not to create adverse long-term effects on the gradual acceptance and practice of family planning as a matter of individual choice. This is where the lawyer's skills might best be brought into play in devising incentives offered by the law for adoption of family planning techniques rather than in devising punishments for the non-adoption of such techniques. Income tax laws provide a perfect example, since incentive schemes could well be worked into the tax system to either encourage people to refrain from marriage or to limit their families. To be realistic, however, incentives offered through the tax system can have, at best, peripheral impact since it is precisely the non-income tax paying group in India that is most in need of such incentives. The legal profession in India must also help in the undertaking of the type of socio-legal empirical studies which are needed before social legislation can be enacted.

Studies of the implementation (or non-implementation) of certain laws such as the criminal law regarding abortion or the Child Marriage Restraint Act will help reveal the social climate prevailing and thereby enable legislators to realistically estimate the degree of acceptance by the society of proposals such as this note deals with.

Lawyers must also take the initiative as regards securing for India a Uniform Civil Code. The absence of a uniform set of laws relating to marriage, divorce, maintenance and other aspects of domestic relations, has made it very difficult for the government to implement its population control programs in the manner they would like to. To give just one example, the Jana Sangh political party in India contends that more Hindus than Muslims (in relation to their respective total populations) are being sterilized.

They further point out that while Hindus are bound by a law which prescribes monogamy, Muslims are permitted under their law to have as many as four wives. The Jana Sangh argument therefore runs along the following lines. The total population of Hindus is likely to dwindle while that of the Muslims is likely to increase. Since in a democracy numbers matter and since in India many votes are cast on the basis of religious and caste loyalties, the present family planning program might eventually change the entire complexion of the Indian nation. The adoption of a uniform set of marriage laws in India would help considerably in countering this argument.

Unfortunately, because of the amount of emotionalism that has been drawn into the entire issue of a Uniform Civil Code for all Indians, such a uniform set of marriage laws seems at the present moment to be almost Utopian. Lawyers, however, could play an invaluable role in helping extract some of the emotionalism from this issue. A comparative study of the various systems of marriage laws prevailing in India could lead to a sufficiently significant body of common principles shared by all of those systems. Such a body of common principles could well constitute the foundation upon which a uniform set of laws, acceptable to members of all religious communities, could be erected.

It would not be an overstatement to declare that the range of skills and perspectives that a lawyer could bring into a population control program in India are limited only by the lawyer's own personal limitations. Population control programs in India cannot but benefit from drawing upon the expertise of legal sociologists.

POPULATION POLICY AND LAW IN ETHIOPIA

*By Worku Tafara**

If Africa is still the "unknown continent" [1] then Ethiopia is its most hidden part. Ethiopia has never conducted nationwide population inquiries, and as a result, even the most recent comprehensive treatments of African demography have little information to communicate on Ethiopia.

In his book entitled *Population, Migration and Urbanization in Africa*, W. A. Hance has repeatedly drawn attention to this lack of information as follows:

> Some data are available for almost all (African) countries. The most serious deficiencies are the estimates for Ethiopia, Somalia and Nigeria. [2] The population patterns of Ethiopia must remain somewhat obscure until a national census has been held. [3] It is not possible to assess the extent of population pressure on the high lands of Ethiopia, though evidence exists that it affects some regions. [4]

Due to such dearth of information, therefore, this paper will have to be limited to a brief discussion of official attitudes towards population as implied in Ethiopia's Third Five Year Plan and to a short report of laws that affect population.

Population Policy

African religions and social structures and African sentiments in general strongly favor high fertility, [5] and Ethiopia is no

*Graduate student, Northwestern University.

1. L. Baumgartner, "Family Planning Around the World," in Family Planning and Population Programs 278 (B. Berelson ed. 1966).
2. W. Hance, Population, Migration and Urbanization in Africa 12 (1970).
3. Id. at 13.
4. Id. at 404.
5. See L. Baumgartner, supra note 1, at 284; see also N. Frothingham, Report to the Pathfinder Fund on Population Concerns and Family Planning in Africa: South of the Sahara 76-106 (January, 1968).

exception. Nevertheless, as many as nine African countries have, in recent years, adopted national population programs as part of their development schemes.[6] Fourteen other countries either support or approve private family planning programs even though they have announced no official national population policies.[7] The rest, which are mainly composed of the sub-Sahara Franco-phonic African countries, remain indifferent or seem to resist the idea of population control.[8]

Ethiopia seems to fit none of the above categorizations very well. Strictly speaking Ethiopia has announced no official government policy. Nevertheless, its planners have relied, as indeed they must, on population estimates which were based on conjecture and have taken the rather optimistic position expressed in the following statement:

> Ethiopia is fortunate in that both the size and the density of her population are highly favourable for economic and social development. The population is estimated at only 24 million and given the area of the country (1,221000 km^2) the density is consequently low compared to many developing countries. The nation offers a potentially large internal market and a large reservoir of manpower which can supply specialized skills for the development of the various sectors of the economy. However, rapid population growth will present problems in the more distant future. At present over half a million people are being added to the population every year. In recent years considerable effort had been made to establish basic health services, to control communicable diseases and to improve the environmental health conditions of the people. With the expansion of these services and the improvement of nutritional levels, it is anticipated that within a single generation there will be a substantial lowering of the death rate. The consequent increase of population will mean that there will be still more mouths to feed, and more children to go to school. To provide for the needs

6. See generally, International Planned Parenthood Federation, Family Planning in Five Continents 1-11 (1970).
7. Id.
8. Id.

of this increasing population, development must therefore be accelerated... [9]

No one is equipped with better information to agree or disagree with the optimism expressed in the above statement. Nevertheless, a number of questions must be raised. One immediate question is the wisdom of the planners' choice of the traditional measure of density, e.g. the ratio of population over area, as the measure of over-population. One wonders if the planners would have arrived at the conclusion, that population is a problem of a "more distant future," had they chosen a different test and examined the critical imbalance between population increase and economic growth, which seems to be manifested by the increasingly conspicuous shortage of schools, the ever-rising unemployment, and the generally low (one of the lowest in Africa) standard of living, now prevailing in Ethiopia.

Further, by the planners' own candid admission, Ethiopia's economy is very depressed. A generation's effort at development has brought little change to the living condition of the average Ethiopian. Eight out of ten people live essentially as their fathers and their forefathers did. Agricultural production now comes largely from small peasant farms providing little more than subsistence. The effect of all this, according to the planners, is low productivity, low savings capacity and a low standard of living for the mass of the Ethiopian people. [10] No one, to be sure, will disagree with the planners' proposal that development must be accelerated in order to provide for the needs of the increasing population. One wonders, however, if Ethiopia's economy, depressed as it is, could be made to accelerate at a rate sufficiently high to offset the effects of unchecked population growth and at the same time meet, as the planners desire it to meet, the fundamental aim of raising the level of per capita production and income so that within a generation the standard of living of the Ethiopian people will be materially improved. The performance of Ethiopia's economy in the past does not suggest that this could be achieved. The planners' optimistic reliance on strenuous efforts in the economic sphere alone to achieve these objectives and their failure to suggest some course of action on the population growth

9. Imperial Ethiopian Government, Third Five Year Development Plan, Parts I and II (mimeograph) at 1-3, 1-4, (1968).

10. Id.

as well is, therefore, quite difficult to explain and may perhaps prove to be regrettable in the long run. Indeed since the planners seem to be satisfied with the present size of the population and its growth rate, and since they anticipate a decline in the crude death rate as health services increase, one would logically have expected them to propose, in addition to accelerated efforts in the economic sphere, a program which would bring about a corresponding decline in the birth rate, so that a constant rate of growth may be maintained. [11]

Laws Affecting Population

Attention shall now be turned to laws that affect population. Next to sub-Sahara Franco-phone African countries, Ethiopia has one of the most conservative and anti-birth control set of laws in Africa. The legal tradition in this respect is best demonstrated by the following provisions of the Fetha Nagast, "the Law of Kings," which, until recent modernization and codification, has been the applicable law in Ethiopia for many centuries. [12]

> ...If a woman conceives and gives her consent to aborting what is in her womb, she shall be beaten and exiled... [13]
>
> If two men have a quarrel and strike a pregnant woman, so that the fetus in the womb comes out, if the spirit does not move in the aborted fetus the one who struck the woman must compensate her husband...but if the spirit is in the fetus (and it dies) life must pay for life, unless amends are made and they are reconciled. [14]
>
> Prohibitation against shedding the seed outside the uterus of the woman...is based on the books and on reason. The first (reason) because the primary end of marriage is the leaving of offsprings... The second...because the word of God who said in the Law

11. Id.
12. The Fetha Nagast, "The Law of Kings" is a collection of Laws first written around 1235-1243 and believed to have been introduced into Ethiopia during the reign of Zer'a Ya'quob (1434-1468).
13. See Fetha Nagast, The Law of the Kings 299 (P. Strauss ed. 1968).
14. Id. at 295.

> that one who lies down with a woman and removes his seed from her shall not escape from death...avoiding the natural fruit...is worse than destroying those who exist... [15]

The age of marriage under the Fetha Nagast was twenty years for a man but only twelve years for a woman. A number of provisions prohibited sexual intercourse between spouses on holy days and days of fasting and during prescribed periods of confinement and of widowhood. Considering the large number of holy days and days of fasting, these restrictions may have had unintended tendencies towards promoting birth control and healthy child spacing although the restrictions were in fact subordinate to an even stronger "prohibition against refusing (to give the conjugal debt owed to) each other." [16]

To the extent that the provisions of the modern civil and penal codes, which shall be discussed hereafter, are based on tradition, the above was the only background available and, as we shall see, the improvements introduced by these modern codes are, at best, very modest. Under the Civil Code, for example, the age of majority for both a man and a woman is 18 years, [17] but, while the age of marriage for a man is the same as the age of majority, it is only fifteen years for a woman and under special circumstances a woman can legally marry at as low an age as 13 years. [18] Furthermore, since opposition to marriage in violation of these provisions could only be made by a limited number of family representatives and/or the public prosecutor, [19] they remain generally unenforced because marriages, legal or illegal, are usually arranged by the family and the public prosecutor is either uninformed or too busy to be concerned about it. Marriage at an age earlier than the legal minimum of 15 or 13 years is, therefore, quite common, particularly in rural Ethiopia. And as the code has dropped all forms of ancient restrictions against sexual intercourse, except the observance of a period of widowhood, [20]

15. Id. at 146-147.
16. Id. at 137-147.
17. Civil Code of the Empire of Ethiopia of 1960, art. 198 (hereinafter Civ. C.)
18. Civ. C., art. 581.
19. Civ. C., art. 592.
20. Civ. C., art. 496.

the net gain, in terms of postponement of early marriages and child spacing, introduced by the modern Civil Code is hardly discernable.

Before entering into a discussion of penal provisions, it is proper to briefly glance at tax and other laws that may affect population. Tax and welfare legislation in most countries tends to support high fertility by alleviating the economic burden which results from having a large family. In this respect Ethiopia is an exception. All persons, unfortunately in some other respects, are equally taxed. No tax rebate or deduction, on the basis of family size, is allowed. A man with six children would, therefore, pay the same tax as a bachelor of the same income. Welfare benefits are practically nonexistent. There is a government pension scheme for civil servants but this too is not graduated on the basis of family size, although minor children of a deceased civil servant, legitimate or illegitimate, and without any limit in number, are entitled to draw from the pension fund.

Illegal abortion is severely dealt with under the Penal Code. If abortion is procured by the pregnant woman herself, the penalty is simple imprisonment from three months to five years. Accomplices and co-offenders are more or less subjected to the same treatment. If abortion is procured by another person, then the penalty is rigorous imprisonment of up to five years, if the woman has freely consented, and rigorous imprisonment from three to ten years if the woman did not freely consent or was incapable of giving her consent. Where the offender acted for gain or where he has habitually made a profession out of abortion, a fine is imposed in addition to the last above mentioned penalty. If the offender is a professional, e.g. doctor, nurse, etc., prohibition of practice may in addition be ordered for either a limited period or for life depending on how often the offense has been repeated.[21]

Therapeutic abortion is recognized under the code, but it is shrouded by many cumbersome legal requirements. The termination of the pregnancy must be necessary to save the pregnant woman from a grave and permanent danger to life or health which is impossible to avert in any other way. The danger to be averted must be diagnosed and certified in writing by a registered medical practitioner. A second doctor, qualified as a

21. See Penal Code of the Empire of Ethiopia of 1952, arts. 529-531 (hereinafter Pen. C.).

specialist in the alleged defect of health and empowered by the competent authority to issue authorization, must concur, after independent examination where necessary, with the findings of the examining physician. And finally a duly substantiated consent of the pregnant woman, or, if she is incapacitated, that of her next of kin or legal representative, must be obtained. [22]

Nonobservance of any of these legal conditions, "except in grave and imminent danger which can be averted only by an immediate intervention," would subject the doctor to the same penalty as that prescribed for an illegal abortion and it is explicitly provided that the defense of professional duty will be of no avail. Both the doctor terminating the pregnancy and the authorizing specialist must subsequently report the abortion to the competent authorities. Failure to do so would entail a penalty of fine or arrest and under certain circumstances even the loss of the right to exercise one's profession. Here again it is provided that the defense of professional secrecy may not be invoked. [23]

Abortion on social grounds, e.g. termination of pregnancy "on account of an exceptionally grave state of physical or mental distress, especially following rape or incest, or because of extreme poverty," is considered as a mitigating factor only. [24] The presence of these extenuating circumstances may, in the discretion of the judge, result in drastic reductions of the severe penalties described above.

There is no provision in the penal code which directly deals with the question of sterilization. "Maiming," however, part of a general offense of causing bodily injury against which the consent of the victim, although a mitigating factor, is no defense. [25] Does voluntary sterilization constitute maiming? To the knowledge of this writer Ethiopian courts did not have an opportunity to pass on the question and this paper will not attempt to speculate an answer.

There is no prohibition against the use or sale of any form of contraceptive devices, but the advertising or public display of contraceptive samples is an offense punishable by fine or arrest not exceeding one month. The offer for sale and the advertising of

22. Pen. C., art. 534.
23. Pen. C., arts. 535-536.
24. Pen. C., art. 533.
25. Pen. C., art. 537.

means or products designed to cause abortion are also similarly treated.[26]

Conclusion

The restrictiveness of the laws affecting population should not be of great consequence. These laws can be reformed, with relative ease, if the requirements of general welfare dictate it.[27] Even under present circumstances a private Family Guidance Association, assisted by a number of international organizations, is extending family planning services to the public "as part of maternal and child health services..." without any governmental or other interference.[28]

The official attitude of the Government, discussed above, however should cause much more concern. Inasmuch as it is based on inadequate information and on some questionable assumptions, the attitude taken could be wrong, and, unless soon corrected, could plunge the country into deeper economic difficulties.

But at the root of all this, is the absence of reliable demographic information on the basis of which sound and informed conclusions could be made and appropriate actions could be taken. As a matter of first priority, therefore, it is strongly urged that this be rectified soon by conducting a nation-wide demographic study. Needless to say, the well-meaning efforts of international organizations, both public and private, would be much more effective if initially directed towards the realization of this task.

26. Pen. C., art. 802.

27. See Revised Constitution of Ethiopia, art. 65.

28. See M. Felszer, Family Guidance Association of Ethiopia 27 (1970).

POPULATION MIGRATION PROBLEMS IN NIGERIA

*By Dipo Odujinrin**

The country, Nigeria, is situated on the west coast of Africa, bounded on the south by the Atlantic Ocean, on the north and west by the Republics of Niger and Dahomey and immediately on the east by the Federal Republic of Cameroons. Lying between parallels 4° and 14° North, Nigeria has a total land area of 356,669 square miles and an estimated population of 54,671,000.[1] However, the distribution of this population is highly uneven, and while there are areas which carry over 300 persons per square mile, there are others that are relatively empty.[2] This unevenness is attributable, not to any natural obstacle, but to the influx of people from the rural to the urban areas. Such movements while creating underpopulation in some areas, result in overpopulation and population pressure in other areas. Unfortunately, these movements which constitute one of the three variables[3] in population change have been relatively neglected in population studies.[4] No one can doubt the fact that migration is a thorny problem, especially on the African scene, and it is the purpose of this paper to focus on the causes and effect of these rural-urban movements and what role the law can play in the balanced distribution of people over the vast land area available.

Migratory Factors

Factors influencing migration have been classified as Pull Factors or those associated with the destination area; and Push

*Graduate student, Harvard University.

1. Federal Ministry of Information, Lagos, Nigeria, 1971 Calendar Publication.
2. P.C. Lloyd, Africa in Social Change 20 (1969).
3. The other two being fertility and mortality rates.
4. R.M. Prothero, "Migration in Tropical Africa" in The Population of Tropical Africa 250 (Caldwell and Okonjo eds.).

Factors or those associated with the areas of origin or source.[5] Berg has also listed the major factors determining the individual's decision to migrate as the intensity of his preference for money against leisure; the level of his income from village production; the effort-price of income earnable outside the village.[6] An important pull factor we may take note of is the fact that the urban centers are to an unusual degree the major areas of modernization, and thus constitute the industrial nodes in the country. Since industrial employment is attractive, especially to young men with relatively few opportunities and obligations and provides higher wages, greater chances for acquiring skills, better access to education, and a more intense contact with the modern world of ideas and technology, the young village man sees his future progress in the urban centers, and makes up his mind to migrate to one of the few urban centers in Nigeria.

The introduction of free primary education in several parts of Nigeria has added impetus to the push factors and aided the young village man in easily making up his mind to quit the rural area. It has been suggested that this accelerated schooling, particularly in the countryside, has produced a disequilibrium between expectation and reality which has become a major reason for the flow to the towns.[7] The primary school graduate can no longer conceive of himself working on the farm when he believes he could take up a job with a steady income in the urban center. Robert Descloitres described the situation aptly in this manner:

> Many of those who receive even a primary education feel that farm work is no longer an appropriate occupation. Indeed some youth see the life of the peasant farmer as the most miserable that exists, one which subjects the individual to physical forces beyond his control while town life appears to offer rapid social advance and liberation.[8]

5. E.S. Lee, A Theory of Migration – Demography III, No. I at 47-57 (1966).
6. Berg, Backward-Sloping Labor Supply Functions in Dual Economies, 480.
7. W. A. Lewis, "Unemployment in Developing Countries," 23 World Today 14 (Jan. 1967).
8. Robert Descloitres quoted in W.A. Hance, Population Migration and Urbanization in Africa 181 (1970).

While no one denies the value of education, it would seem that this free primary education scheme has a harmful effect in that it alienates the young village man from the land and makes him have an unrealistic expectation from the urban centers, believing that his education, which no doubt is inadequate, would perform miracles and transform him from a poor village boy to a wealthy urban dweller.

It has, however, been suggested that this migrant-labor system represents an efficient adaptation to the economic environment in West Africa as a whole.[9] It is further stated that the system permitted that sub-region to enjoy more rapid economic growth than would otherwise have been possible and that the system benefits both the labor exporting villages and the recipient areas. It is argued that migration makes good economic sense from the point of view of both the individuals concerned and the economy as a whole. This view seems very difficult to accept. While it is not easy to see the benefit that accrues to the exporting villages, the depletion of the villages of their able-bodied young men results in the gross reduction of the productive capacity of the rural areas on which the urban centers depend for their food consumption. Kay[10] has rightly pointed out that the system of labor migration saps the vigor of the population in the rural areas and indeed presents serious problems to those anxious to develop those areas.

The benefit to the recipient areas is not always visible; on the other hand, great social problems have been created as a result of the heavy influx of young people from the rural to the urban areas. The pitiable social condition of these new arrivals in the urban areas has been vividly described in the following manner:

> The point that must be stressed in referring to this suffering mass of humanity displaced from the rural areas to the filthy peripheries of the great cities, is that few of them experience the 'transition' from agricultural to urban industrial labor called for by the mechanism of development and the model of modernisation. They are neither housed, nor trained, nor employed, nor serviced.

9. Berg, The Economics of the Migrant Labor System 160, 181.
10. Kay, "The Distribution of African Population in Southern Rhodesia: Some Preliminary Notes," Rhodes-Livingstone Communication No. 18 (Lusaka 1964).

> They languish on the urban periphery without entering into any productive relationship with its industrial operations. These are the 'Displaced Persons,' the displaced persons of the developmental process... a human flotsam and jetsam that has been displaced from traditional agricultural life without being incorporated into modern industrial life.[11]

One can only conclude from this, therefore, that rather than being a benefit either to the recipient areas or to the individuals concerned, this rural-urban labor movement is a very harmful system that has not only ruined lives of potentially capable people, but has deprived the economy as a whole of the participation of otherwise economically active people needed desperately for economic growth, and created a human flotsam and jetsam who have become a public charge on the State.

This indiscriminate migration of the younger generation from the rural to the urban areas has also created serious unemployment problems in Nigeria. In 1965, an estimated 34 percent of the laboring force of Lagos was out of work and C.R. Frank, studying the employment-creating aspects of Nigerian development plans has concluded that urban unemployment would become increasingly severe.[12] No one can deny the grave political implications of letting large numbers of frustrated young men lie idle and indeed the rate at which crimes have risen in Nigeria's urban centers has given cause for concern.[13]

What Role Can the Law Play in Restricting This Drift of Young People to Towns?

It has only recently been recognized by the various governments in Africa that agricultural development is a necessary concomitant to industrial development. While the industries need

11. D. Lerner, "Comparative Analysis of Processes of Modernisation," in The City in Modern Africa 24 (Minor ed.)
12. C. R. Frank, Jr., "Industrialization and Employment Generation in Nigeria," 9 The Nigerian Journal of Economic and Social Studies No. 3, at 277-297 (Nov. 1967).
13. This has led to the setting up of special courts to hear cases involving armed robbery punishable by death.

the raw materials which come from "the land," they also need markets for their products which largely subsistence-farming hinterlands do not provide. With this late realization, these governments have been making laws in an attempt to restrict the in-migration to the cities and create a stable and vigorous labor force on the fields. Unfortunately, the various measures adopted have not been very effective. For example, the Republic of Niger passed a law in 1962 requiring all unemployed urban youths to perform some service or return to their native villages. Of course, this type of measure was ineffectual and the police were reported in April 1963 as having rounded up all such youths in Niamey and shipped them back to the country; again in June 1964, the government ordered all unemployed men to take up agricultural work on pain of being prosecuted as vagabonds, [14] this again was not successful. A similar measure was adopted in the Central African Republic, where a decree was passed in 1964 directing all unsalaried citizens "living on their wits" in urban centers be rounded up and put to work rehabilitating old plantations. It was declared that this was not a violation of International Work Conventions, but rather an economic necessity. [15] Related measures for forcibly repatriating the so-called idlers have been adopted by Kenya, Tanzania, Ghana, Tunisia, and Morocco, but with no success. Ivory Coast's measure of creating incentives in the villages has also not met with much success. [16]

While some of these measures are objectionable on moral and other grounds, it is apparent that they cannot succeed in restricting in-migration to the cities as long as the economic structure of these various African states remains what it presently is. In short, until the African states eliminate the dual nature of their economy and integrate the rural subsistence economy into the modern cash economy, all the various measures they take to combat the drift to towns will continue to be fruitless. If there are no resources available any longer for people to work with in the cities, it is only wise to extend the process of modernization into the rural areas. Indeed it has been observed that one of the notable

14. V. Thompson, "Niger" in National Unity and Regionalism in Eight African States 178 (G. Carter ed.).

15. Thompson & Adloff, The Emerging States of French Equatorial Africa 425.

16. W. A. Hance, supra, note 8, at 278-9.

characteristics of many African countries, is the rapid fading away of the signs of modernity as one leaves the urban centers.[17]

The primary cause of unemployment has been attributed to the absence of resources for people to work with, and the remedy for this has been stated to lie in capital formation, which adds new resources, or makes existing resources, e.g. land, more usable.[18] Since most African states may find the burden of adding new resources crushing, the other alternative is to exploit to the maximum, whatever resources they have at their disposal. What we are advocating therefore is the extension of the various laws concerning land tenure which presently operate in Nigeria's urban areas, into the rural areas. Of particular relevance is the Registration of Titles Act[19] which operates presently in Lagos and which makes title to such registered land certain and effective. With such extension, the rural areas will meaningfully be brought under the application of the bankruptcy laws, and hence the various commercial banks will be confident in granting loans to the rural farmers for the purchase of the necessary farm implements, on the security of their land. The present traditional pattern of land rights which usually gives the farmer no power to alienate the land on which his produce grows, has inhibited and will continue to inhibit the banks from granting loans to individual farmers for agricultural development. It is believed that with the consequent commercialization of agriculture, the rural areas will be effectively incorporated within the market economy and there will be the incentive to grow more. There is no gainsaying the fact that this will create more resources for people to work with and will benefit the economy as a whole. The earnings thus generated can also be taxed, yielding added revenue to the Gross National Product. A caveat should, however, be entered here, that this would require great political will since a higher rate of domestic savings can be achieved through such taxation only by force. Japan did it successfully, and there is no doubt that Nigeria can also be successful in doing it, given the necessary political will and tact.[20] In this manner law will also be acting as a vehicle for economic development.

17. Id. at 209.
18. W.A. Lewis, The Theory of Economic Growth in Taxation for African Economic Development 10 (M. Taylor ed.)
19. Ordinance No. 13 of 1935, as amended.
20. W.A. Lewis, supra note 18, at 11.

Conclusion

As observed earlier, the urban centers are the areas of economic activities in most African states. They are also the intellectual and social capitals, the seats of governments, the main focii of political activity of all sorts. [21] In a study of Lagos which has the unique position of being both the capital of Nigeria and the capital of the State of Lagos, it was discovered that the city accounts for about 46 percent of the electricity consumed, 56 percent of the country's telephones, 20 percent of its newspapers, 90 percent of its periodicals, 37 percent of its hospitals and 38 percent of vehicle registrations. It is also Nigeria's leading port, rail and airways center and its single most important industrial node. [22] The resultant effect of this concentration of national activities is that in the intercensal period between 1950 and 1963, its population increased by 188.9 percent. [23] The majority of the migrants in this large increase now constitutes a human flotsam and jetsam of the developmental process.

It is undoubtedly true that with the diversification of national activities into more urban areas created by the infiltration of the rural areas, the population pressure on the few urban centers would be greatly reduced. The creation of more urban centers will also have the indirect effect of reducing fertility rates since the change has been observed in the cities, towards a more intimate and affectionate father-child relationship oriented towards the raising of fewer, more self-directed children. [24] Indeed, it has been asserted that urban living, opportunities of occupational mobility, changing attitudes towards the upbringing of children, the spread of schooling and especially advanced schooling and other social changes would bring about to an increasing degree, pressures essentially similar in kind to those which have led, since the late nineteenth century, to a restriction in the size of the European family. [25]

21. W.A. Hance, supra note 8, at 209.
22. C.N. Ejiogu, African Rural-Urban Migrants in the Main Migrant Areas of the Lagos Federal Territory in supra, note 4, at 320.
23. R.A. Levine, N.H. Klein & C.R. Owen, "Father-child Relationships and Changing Life Styles in Ibadan, Nigeria" in supra note 11, at 252.
24. Caldwell, Population Growth and Family Change in Africa 17-18 (1968).

APPENDIX

Table 1

Technology Tiers	of Method	Methods Generally Available	Family Planning Program Needs
5	1970's?	Methods listed below plus: "a non-toxic and completely effective substance of method which when self-administered on a single occasion would ensure the non-pregnant state at completion of a monthly cycle."	Minimal regulation of sexual activity. Reduced need for education. Main emphasis on ensuring availability of contraceptives and post contraceptives through medical and non-medical facilities.
4	1970's	Methods listed below plus legal surgical abortion.	Slight regulation of sexual activity. Less emphasis on education. Main emphasis on provision of contraceptive services through medical and non-medical facilities and abortion services through medical facilities.
3	1960's	Methods listed below plus intra-uterine devices and oral contra-ceptives.	Some regulation of sexual activity; Continued emphasis on education and pro-vision of contraceptives and family plan-ning services through medical and non-medical facilities.
2	Before 1960	Methods listed below plus, condoms, diaphragms, vaginal chemicals, rhythm, and surgical sterilization.	Considerable regulation of sexual activity; emphasis on education and provision of materials and services through medical and non-medical facilities.
1	Before 1870	Abstinence, coitus interruptus, delayed marriage and non-marriage, crude vaginal barriers (e.g., sponges), douching, and illegal abortion.	Strict regulation of sexual activity. Emphasis on education.

Source: R.T. Ravenholt, P.T. Piotrow, J.J. Speidel, Use of Oral Contraceptives: A Decade of Controversy, 8 Int'l J. Gyn. Obst. 941 (November 1970)

Table 2

PRINCIPAL MEANS OF FERTILITY CONTROL

(By time and by route of administration)

	1968 Preconceptive	1968 Postconceptive	1970 Preconceptive	1970 Postconceptive
Clinical Administration Required	A IUD's Surgical Sterilization Vaginal Diaphragm Oral Contraceptives (in some countries)	B Surgical Abortion Intraamniotic Injection	A IUD's Surgical Sterilization Vaginal Diaphragm Oral Contraceptives (in some countries)	B Surgical Abortion Intraamniotic Injection (Intravenous and intrauterine since January, 1970)
Self Administration Feasible	C Abstinence non-coitus rhythm coitus interruptus Condoms Vaginal sponge, foam, douche, etc. Oral Contaceptives (in some countries)	D	C Abstinence non-coitus rhythm coitus interruptus Condoms Vaginal sponge, foam douche, etc. Oral Contraceptives (insome countries)	D Prostaglandins (Vaginal since September, 1970)

Source: R.T. Ravenholt, J.J. Speidel, Prostaglandins in Family Planning Strategy, 180 Annals N.Y. Acad. Sciences 537 (April 30, 1971).

Figure 1

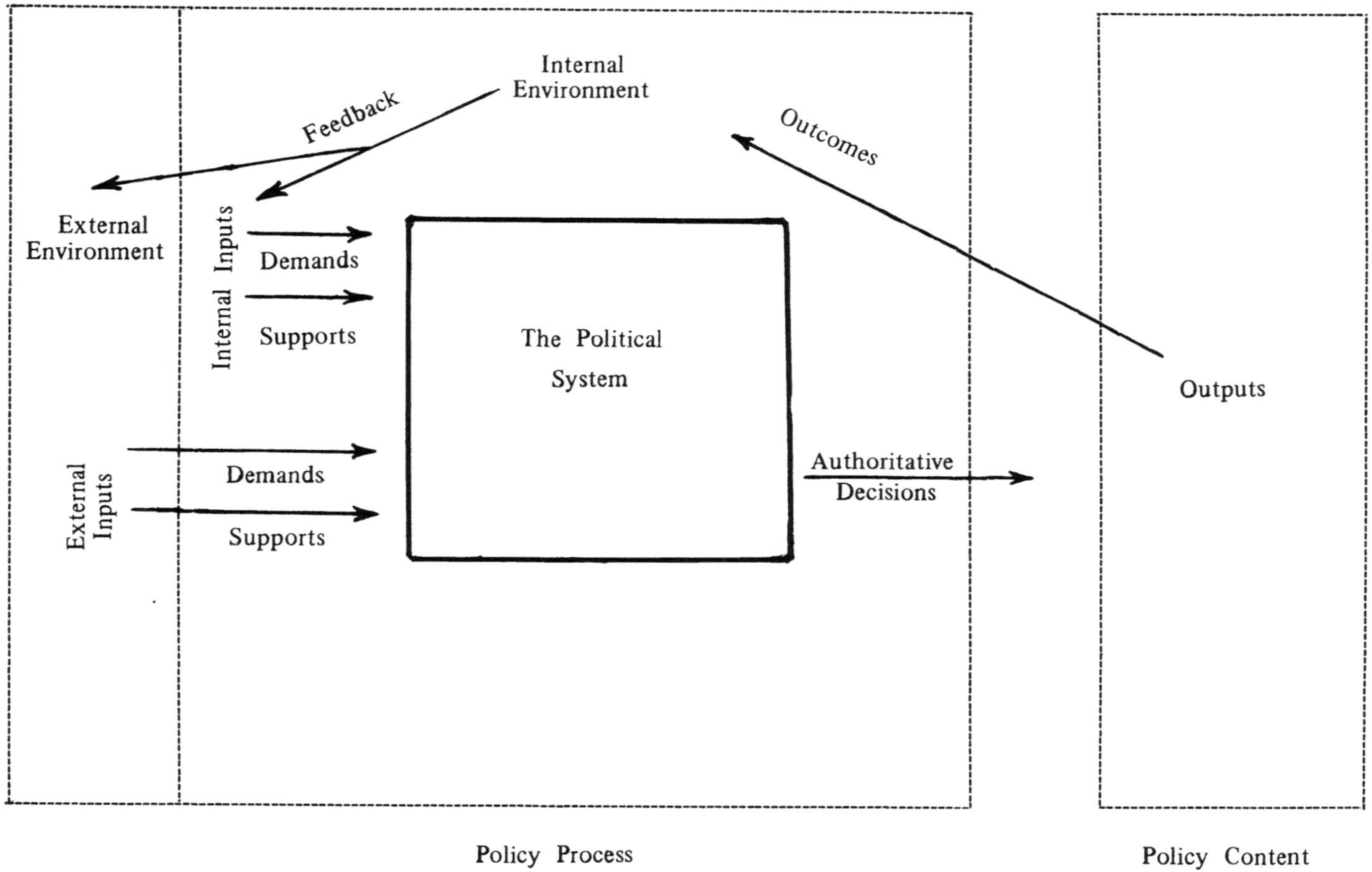

Source: Adapted from A. Ranney, *The Study Of Policy Content,* Political Science and Public Policy 9 (A. Ranney ed. 1968).

Table 3

EXTERNAL ORGANIZATIONS ASSISTING LATIN AMERICAN POPULATION PROGRAMS
(by country)

	Argentina	Bolivia	Brazil	Chile	Colombia	Costa Rica	Cuba	Domin. Rep.	Ecuador	El Salvador	Guatemala	Haiti	Honduras	Mexico	Nicaragua	Panama	Paraguay	Peru	Uruguay	Venezuela	Latin Am
Bilateral--U.S.																					
USAID		O		O	O	O		O	O	O	O		O		O	O	O			O	O
Peace Corps								O		O											
Dept. of State																					O
Miscellaneous	O																		O		O
Bilateral--Other																					
Sweden					O	O	O	O		O	O							O	O		
Netherlands		O	O							O			O			O	O	O		O	
United Kingdom															O						
Multilateral--Int'l.																					
UN Family		O			O	O		O		O	O							O			
World Bank																					O
OECD																					O
Multilateral--Regional																					
CELADE	O			O		O				O	O		O		O	O	O				O

ECLA																					O
PAHO	O		O		O				O									O	O		O
OAS															O						O
IDB																					O
Private--Secular																					
CARE													O		O						
Ford	O		O	O	O	O			O					O				O	O	O	O
IPPF	O		O	O	O	O		O	O	O	O		O	O		O	O	O	O	O	O
Oxford Committee			O	O								O		O							
Pathfinder	O	O	O	O	O	O		O	O	O	O	O	O	O	O	O	O	O	O	O	O
Pop. Council	O		O	O	O	O		O	O	O	O	O	O	O	O	O	O	O	O	O	O
Pop. Crisis Comm.																					O
Pop. Ref. Bureau				O	O																O
Rockefeller					O	O								O				O			O
World Neighbors		O	O		O				O		O	O					O	O			
Miscellaneous																					O
Private--Religious																					
AFSC														O							O
CELAP	O	O		O	O	O		O			O						O	O		O	O
CWS		O	O		O	O		O		O	O	O	O				O				
Miscellaneous		O										O					O				

Table 4

EXTERNAL ORGANIZATIONS ASSISTING LATIN AMERICAN POPULATION PROGRAMS
(by function)

	Local Action	Research	Education and Training	Technical Assistance and Evaluation	Information and Promotion	Financial and Material Assistance
Bilateral–U.S.						
USAID				O	O	O
Peace Corps				O		
Dept. of State					O	
Miscellaneous		O	O	O	O	O
Bilateral--Other						
Sweden				O	O	O
Netherlands						O
United Kingdom				O		O
Multilateral--Int'l.						
UN Family		O	O	O	O	O
World Bank						O
OECD		O			O	
Multilateral–Regional						
CELADE		O	O	O	O	
ECLA		O				
PAHO		O	O	O	O	
OAS				O	O	
IDB					O	O
Private–Secular						
CARE						O
Ford						O
IPPF			O	O	O	O
Oxford Committee						O
Pathfinder			O	O	O	O
Pop. Council		O	O	O	O	O
Pop. Crisis Comm.					O	
Pop. Ref. Bureau					O	
Rockefeller						O
World Neighbors	O			O	O	O
Miscellaneous			O	O	O	
Private--Religious						
AFSC				O	O	O
CELAP		O	O	O	O	
CWS					O	O
Miscellaneous	O					O

www.ingramcontent.com/pod-product-compliance
Ingram Content Group UK Ltd.
Pitfield, Milton Keynes, MK11 3LW, UK
UKHW020820290926
15470UKWH00003B/1270

9 780313 226199